PAYING THE RENT

ADVENTURES OF A
LEFT COAST ACTIVIST LAWYER
FROM THE TURBULENT '60s
TO THE ERA OF DONALD TRUMP

A MEMOIR

DICK EIDEN

LYMER & HART
GARDEN OAK PRESS
Rainbow, California

Lymer & Hart
Garden Oak Press
1953 Huffstatler St., Suite A
Rainbow, CA 92028
760 728-2088
gardenoakpress.com
lymerharts@gmail.com

First published by Lymer & Hart/Garden Oak Press on October 15, 2019.

ISBN-13:   978-1-7323753-5-2
ISBN-10:   1-7323753-5-6

Library of Congress Control Number: 2019948044

Printed in the United States of America

Lymer & Hart is an imprint of Garden Oak Press

Activism is the rent I pay
for living on the planet.

— ALICE WALKER

Contents

PAYING THE RENT

ADVENTURES OF A
LEFT COAST ACTIVIST LAWYER
FROM THE TURBULENT '60S
TO THE ERA OF DONALD TRUMP

A MEMOIR

DICK EIDEN

LYTHER & FINCH

Prologue

When I do bad, I feel bad.
When I do good, I feel good.
That's my religion.

— ABRAHAM LINCOLN

March, 2003

I was asked to speak at a last-minute rally against *Shock and Awe*, President George W. Bush's announced attack on Saddam Hussein and the people of Iraq. When I say "last minute," I don't mean it was thrown together hastily. I mean it was just four days before the bombing and invasion began. Although the White House pretended the U.S. might not attack because Saddam Hussein could still avert war by complying with U.S. demands, everyone knew the war would start soon.

The event was billed as a veterans' rally against this imminent war. I was asked to speak, as the only speaker who was not a veteran of military service. I was among those leading local protests in the six months since war-talk started reaching our consciousness. In May, 2002, I first heard that the President and his advisors were planning to attack Iraq. When I told some friends and family of my concern, they said I was crazy and had finally gone off the deep end. They were right – it did seem insane!

Why would President Bush attack Iraq? Our military had its hands full in Afghanistan, where the war had been going badly for more than a year. And why Saddam Hussein? He was a terrible dictator, but he had been the U.S.'s close friend and ally during the recent (1980-88) Iran-Iraq war. And the U.S. supported many dictators across the world and throughout our history, so why invade and overthrow this one? Saddam had nothing to do with the September 11 attack or Osama Bin Laden. In fact, Bin Laden hated Saddam Hussein because he was secularizing Iraq. War on Iraq couldn't be true.

But it was.

The White House claimed Saddam Hussein possessed Weapons of Mass Destruction (WMD) and posed a threat to the region. But there was a great deal of evidence the White House was lying.

For one thing, U.N. weapons inspectors had access to potential weapons sites since George H.W. Bush's 1991 Gulf War. They didn't think Iraq had any such facilities. One of the top inspectors, Scott Ritter, was a former U.S. Marine with impeccable credentials. The lead inspector, Mohamed ElBaradei, was an Egyptian legal scholar, widely respected as a diplomat and honest broker. Both men were convincing about having access to Iraq and having found none of the chemical, biological or nuclear weapons facilities the White House claimed were there.

Journalists from Knight-Ridder were reporting the truth: the White House was making up excuses for a decision it made long ago. But their stories were drowned out by the big media outlets, which repeated government press releases and sources. Even the leading Knight-Ridder newspaper – *The Philadelphia Enquirer* – refused to report the real story being uncovered by its own reporters. In short, many people knew the government was lying in order to get us involved in another tragic war, and they let it happen.

Media heavyweights and Democrats in Congress joined Republicans to overwhelm the opposition to the imminent war in Iraq. The usual combination of fear and patriotic myths about the importance and virtue of our mission characterized what President Bush would label "a crusade." Acknowledging the lack of evidence of WMD, National Security Advisor and later Secretary of State Condoleezza Rice famously told Wolf Blitzer on CNN, "We don't want the smoking gun to be a mushroom cloud."[1]

The Bush Administration did all it could to downplay the cost of the war. Vice President Dick Cheney claimed that Iraq's oil wealth would pay for this war. He also predicted that U.S. forces would be "greeted as liberators."[2] He was wrong on both counts.

This would be quick war, the White House promised, lasting only a few days or weeks. As I write this in 2019, U.S. troops remain in Iraq, in a combat zone, in harm's way.

But the veterans on the stage with me in March, 2003 knew first-hand why starting a war without adequate justification was declared a war crime at the 1948 Nuremberg Trials and Nuremberg Conventions – international rules of war that our country had taken the lead in creating. Many German and Japanese leaders were condemned and executed for such crimes after WWII pursuant to these rules, which our leaders were now about

5

to violate. The veterans knew that war was unpredictable and death was arbitrary, killing any and all.

In the months leading up to this day, we picketed and rallied, wrote Letters to the Editor, held educational events, film showings and poetry readings to inform and unite enough opposition to stop the war. One Sunday I stood up in church and said I had picket signs in my car and was going to a busy corner to stand for an hour after church. Fourteen people joined me that morning.

But in early March, the timetable for war was clear, and we had pretty much given up hope of preventing it. Still, we did our best against the odds. This last-ditch effort hoped to talk some sense into the American public and/or Congress. Maybe it would just make us feel better, but that felt necessary in such a dark time.

Eight speakers and an emcee sat on folding chairs on the stage of the Oceanside Pier Amphitheater, bordering Camp Pendleton, where scores of young Marines would soon find themselves in the sands of Iraq. The audience could see the beach and ocean behind the band shell. It was a beautiful day. The other seven spoke first, introducing themselves as having served in one branch or another of the military, and most in combat. It was very moving to hear these diverse veterans testify from the heart that war was serious business that routinely killed civilians, and therefore required extreme justification and careful verification.

One speaker had served in WWII. Most were my age and had served in Vietnam. Two were veterans of George H.W. Bush's 1991 Gulf War, which had decimated Saddam Hussein's military with air power and ships at sea. Among their introductory credentials, each noted how many years they served in the military.

As the last speaker, I began by stating my name and saying, "I'm a veteran of the peace movement– and I'm a lifer."

I reiterated the main message of the rally: there was no reason for this war. And it would be a costly disaster for the U.S. and the Middle East. I said I was confident that no honest judge would sign a probable cause warrant for this war based on the evidence provided by the White House.

I pointed out that wars waged by every government were always preceded and justified by an avalanche of propaganda about how evil the enemy was, how we had no choice, and by one big juicy lie, like: *Remember the Maine*, the Gulf of Tonkin attack, or that Kuwait nursery story used to justify George H.W. Bush's 1991 air war on Iraq.

I was on the podium that day because I was one of the few people in the area with experience attending and organizing protests. I attended hundreds of protests since 1965 and helped organize dozens. But there was a lull in mass protests since the Reagan years, and people had forgotten.

I typed up detailed instructions about making effective but inexpensive picket signs and emailed them to hundreds of people on my email list. I tried to centralize information about the war, anti-war speakers, and activities. I knew how to get a permit when one was needed. I understood other legal and logistics issues, and helped organize protests at the beach, in parks, outside malls, and in downtown Vista, where I lived.

In addition to making some comments, I would usually read one or more poems at these events. My favorite was *War* by Carl Sandberg. At a small candle-light vigil on a corner in downtown Vista the night before the war started, I read *War* and reminded people how in *Star Wars*, Princess Leia was forced to watch as her home planet Alderaan was blown to bits by the Death Star. Far away, Obie Wan Kenobi stumbles next to Luke Skywalker. Stunned, Obie Wan reveals he sensed "a great disturbance in the force, as if millions of voices cried out in terror, and were suddenly silenced."

What President G.W. Bush called *Shock and Awe* would kill many Iraqi people in the days to come. The bombing began on March 19.

This book tells how I came to be an experienced and scarred veteran of the movement for peace and social justice, speaking out against another war on that stage alongside military veterans. It's the story of my transformation from a middle-class white kid of conservative parents who grew up in the '50s and became a long-haired leftist anti-war protestor and draft dodger, a full participant in The Sixties, and a lifelong activist in *The Movement* for social change.

---

[1] Discussing Iraqi President Saddam Hussein's nuclear capabilities, January, 10, 2003.

[2] *Meet the Press*, March 16, 2003.

Straight Outta Pomona

I grew up in a new tract home in suburban Southern California in the 1950's. My parents were Minnesota people who had come west during WWII and stayed. My dad worked at the Kaiser Steel plant in Fontana, and mom was a secretary in Pomona, where the three of us lived in middle-class nirvana.

I didn't know much about anything until I went away to college in 1963, when the era we call The Sixties really began. That June, our high school graduation was held, like many before it, at the Pomona Fairgrounds racetrack with Mt. Baldy and the San Gabriel mountains as a backdrop. We didn't know it, but America would go through some big changes almost immediately.

The Martin Luther King, Jr. *I have a dream* speech, during the March on Washington, happened that August, the assassination of JFK that November, and three months later, the first American appearance of the Beatles on the Ed Sullivan show. Those milestones are as good a starting point for The '60s as any cluster of events. Few people had any idea what the decade of '63 – '73 would hold.

My friends and I came of age during the build-up of U.S. troops in Vietnam in 1963 – from 900 in 1960 to 16,300, then to 536,100 in 1968, the most explosive year of the era. And my first year in law school. And the year I lost my student deferment.

The Civil Rights Movement gained strength and influence since the mid-1950s. The war in Vietnam was becoming big news. The Cold-War nuclear showdown with the Soviet Union had people both on edge and divided. We didn't know it, but the U.S. was headed for an internal showdown that would tear the country apart and estrange many of us from our families and each other.

Heating up since the mid-Fifties, the Civil Rights Movement ignited widespread activism in the early '60's: lunch counter sit-ins in Greensboro, North Carolina in 1960, Freedom Rides in 1961, the March on Washington in 1963,

Mississippi Freedom Summer (voter registration) in 1964, the Civil Rights Act of 1964, Bloody Sunday in Selma and the Voting Rights Act in 1965, and more.

These struggles for equality – and the brutal resistance of white mobs and the Jim Crow system – had a huge impact on many people, and gave birth to the Black Liberation Movement.

In May, 1967, 20 black leather and beret-clad, shotgun and rifle-toting Black Panthers went to California's State Capital to protest a bill that would restrict citizens from carrying loaded weapons. With a crowd of journalists following, they went into the capitol building, where leader Bobby Seale proclaimed Mandate #1: "As the aggression of the racist American government escalates in Vietnam, the police agencies of America escalate the repression of black people throughout the ghettos. . .the time has come for black people to arm themselves against this terror before it's too late."

This statement coincided with my own political awakening. The issues of war and black liberation dominated my life since college. Who knew?

I wasn't at the state capital on that day, but a few months earlier I had been in Sacramento with U.C. students from all over the state, to urge legislators to keep tuition low so that working-class kids like me would still have a chance at a good education. A small group of us met with newly-elected assemblyman Pete Schabarum, who bristled at my comment that he rode into the statehouse on Ronald Reagan's coattails. I was young, and that's what I had heard. Thinking it was common knowledge, I didn't expect he'd be offended. But he didn't see it that way. What did I know?

In the early '60s many black and white students went to the South and became radicalized by the brutal struggle to register black voters and integrate lunch counters, and by the confrontation tactics being developed, often on the spot. They brought a new consciousness back to their campuses each fall after 1961, helping transform colleges and universities, mocked as hotbeds of apathy, into centers of unrest and activism by the mid-'60s – the cutting edge of what would become known as *The Movement*.

At first, the activism back home concerned student issues: free speech on campus, dress codes, curfews, separation of men and women in living facilities – all part of *in loco parentis*, the school acting as parent – as well as segregation and other limitations on blacks on some campuses, the content of classes, undemocratic decision-making processes, and more.

With leadership from the veterans of summer civil rights struggles, '60s student activism could be said to have begun with the Port Huron Statement by Tom Hayden and other Students for a Democratic Society (SDS) supporters from the University of Michigan in 1962. Student unrest didn't burst on the national scene, however, until fall 1964, when Jack Weinberg, Mario Savio and others returned from the South and tried to distribute "outside" literature on the U.C. Berkeley campus. Jack was arrested in Sproul Plaza and placed in a police car, which was quickly surrounded by students who wouldn't let it leave with Jack inside. This started a long series of arrests, school disciplinary actions, protests, negotiations, agreements and agreements broken, which lasted for months in what became known as the Free Speech Movement (FSM).

The rebellion and unrest at Cal Berkeley created national headlines partly because the same issues and nascent activism were at play across the country.

Although *The Movement* would eventually become loud, rowdy, creative, colorful and transformative, we were never a majority on campuses or anywhere else. Between 1965 and 1968, only about two to three percent of students considered themselves activists. Only about 20% participated in protests. Most students wanted to be like their parents, play it safe, get steady, good paying jobs, have a family, and stay out of trouble.

An avalanche of propaganda from parents, authority figures, government, media, and clergy preached patriotism, respect for authority, the American way of life, the goodness of our mission, the purity of our motives, the evil and cruelty of our enemies.

The Fifties had been largely dominated by the Red Scare, searching for communists and "fellow travelers" everywhere. People had to sign loyalty oaths for many jobs. Government hearings, like the House Un-American Activities Committee (HUAC) and similar state tribunals forced people to name their political friends and family members or go to jail, like novelist Howard Fast and the Hollywood Ten, or leave the country, like writers Dalton Trumbo and Michael Wilson. Afraid not to fit in, people became active in a church, a service club, a sports team. They avoided talking about politics for fear of saying something controversial and getting on a list.

Another big issue in The Fifties – juvenile delinquency – baffled the WWII generation, which was ill-equipped to handle it. That generation grew up during The Depression, served in the military as young adults during WWII, and had little time for big questions like the meaning of life or the direction of society. They were raised in survival mode, forced to work together and obey authority. They thought that's how their kids should and would be.

But us kids, like all kids, were often unruly, didn't always agree or obey, broke some rules. We didn't feel the same need for security and success that our parents did.

An old Jewish proverb says, "Do not confine your children to your learning. They were born in a different time." We wanted more out of life than a paycheck and a cookie-cutter house with a white picket fence.

Our contempt for respectability was expressed in 1965 by artists like the Beatles' *Nowhere Man*, Bob Dylan's *Ballad of the Thin Man*, and, of course, *The Times They Are A'Changin'*.

12

My friends and I couldn't know all the history, of course, much less understand the dynamics at play, but a critical mass of young people was beginning to rebel against the enforced patriotism and suffocating conformity of the 1950's. The rumblings of discontent were not heard by most people until they became impossible to ignore.

When it arrived, *The Movement* became like a train. You had three choices: get on it, or curse the noise, smoke and traffic disruption, or wave and cheer as it passed by.

Our generation was torn apart by the divisions that were being created and revisited every day at work and school, at Thanksgiving, Christmas, and Hanukkah, when we argued with family members, friends, and co-workers about the war in Vietnam, the Civil Rights struggle, marijuana, long hair, protests, rock music.

And there were serious consequences to the choices we made. The public and the "establishment" – an admittedly imprecise, but still descriptive term – were trapped in WWII and Cold War mode. A September, 1966 poll showed that 75% of the public supported the war in Vietnam. After President Johnson ordered the bombing of oil depots at Hanoi and Haiphong, 80% supported the action. And of those who didn't support the war, only a tiny handful protested. Most still considered protest as unpatriotic.

The atmosphere was so jingoistic that violence was encouraged by so-called "responsible" society. *The Christian Century* declared "Open Season on Dissenters." California's Democrat Governor Edmund G. "Pat" Brown said protests "gave aid and comfort to Hanoi." The *Chicago Tribune* urged the government to "act in the toughest way possible," and the Jackson, Mississippi *Daily News* said, "This is the time for police brutality if there ever was one." With opinion leaders talking like that, it would come as no surprise that war supporters held signs proclaiming "More Police Brutality," "Burn the Teach-In Professors," "Burn Yourselves, Not Your Draft Cards." [1]

Indeed, peace demonstrations and protesters were physically attacked in Cleveland, Ann Arbor, Austin, Boston, and New York City. Students got expelled from schools and colleges, arrested and put in chains at Michigan State. Conservative politicians in Georgia didn't allow duly-elected Julian Bond to be seated as a state representative in 1966 because he opposed the war (and he was black). [1]

A peace activist was beaten to death in Rochester, New York, an activist shot to death in Richmond, California, and a Detroit anti-war office invaded and trashed, leaving one dead, two wounded by shotgun fire. [1]

The divisions of that era fell out along other lines as well. Conservative whites never understood or accepted the Civil Rights movement, and even conservative blacks disapproved of militant tactics. The public felt that "this whole protest thing" was contrary to the WWII ethos of respecting authority, doing your bit, not making waves. Conservatives came to hate everything about *The Movement*: long hair, casual clothing, tie-dye, incense, and marijuana, which became an excuse to put young people in jail and shut them up.

Conservative politicians and opinion-makers even condemned rock music. It led to sex, drugs, and juvenile delinquency – as if nobody had been drunk or had had sex before rock music. And these authority figures thought they had plenty of proof, because young people were listening to "that music," then "acting up" at home, on campus, and in the streets. There had to be a connection!

Another thing: their lily-white kids were going to racially mixed clubs and listening and dancing to black artists and that sexy, unruly "devil music." Their greatest nightmare was our idea of heaven – young people of all colors smoking pot, dancing, and talking about peace.

Yes, we were young, idealistic, and there was, indeed, "a whole lotta shakin' goin' on."

For all these reasons and more, many of us rebelled.

I was in college and law school in Southern California from 1963 to 1970, and I had the freedom to be involved in some of the most tumultuous, mind-blowing, and game-changing years of the 20th century.

With those years as my launching pad, I wound up staying involved in *The Movement* for the rest of my life.

[1]*The Movement and the Sixties: Protest **in** America from Greensboro to Wounded Knee*, by Terry H. Anderson {Oxford University Press: 1996 [5th Edition]), pp. 144 -151

I

COLLEGE
IN THE '60s

We must learn to see the world anew.

— *ALBERT EINSTEIN*

The Life of Riley

When my friends and I graduated from Pomona High School in 1963, the '50s era was still largely in place. Most adults had been through the Great Depression in the 1930's and World War II in the '40's, now had jobs and young children, and were more than ready for peace, prosperity and stability. President Eisenhower went from being a leader among war leaders to a smiling, grandfatherly figure, frequently shown playing golf, a signal that hard times were over and it was OK to relax and enjoy yourself.

Thousands of families migrated to Southern California from the dust bowl and depression in the 30's, and many more left rural and Midwest communities for the coasts and big cities during WWII. My parents, Ray Eiden and Mae Moline Eiden, grew up and were married in Minnesota in early 1941. Anticipating the war, my dad joined the Navy in April and they spent most of WWII in Bremerton, Washington. Dad was eventually transferred to Mare Island Navy base in San Francisco Bay, where I was born in the Navy hospital in 1945. Like many WWII veterans, my parents decided to stay in the west. I was five months old when dad was discharged and we settled in Southern California.

The '50s have a well-deserved reputation for conformity, or "keeping up with the Joneses". Newcomers to Southern California took off their dusty farm clothes and military uniforms and strove for the appearance of respectability and normality. Couples wanted a nice house in a nice neighborhood, a well-kept yard, a picket fence, and a nice car in the driveway. They wanted their nice children to be well dressed, well groomed, and well behaved. These were visible signs that no matter where they were from, "we're as good as anybody".

Popular culture offered up families like *Ozzie and Harriet* and *Father Knows Best* as examples of how to live in this new, middle-class, suburban America. The dad got a haircut every week or two and usually wore a coat and tie – even after work when he sat in his chair smoking his pipe and reading the afternoon newspaper. The mom was always nicely dressed, cheerful, and had dinner in the oven when dad got home from work.

The Life of Riley was like the other two shows except Chester A. Riley worked on the line in an aircraft plant, came home in work clothes carrying a lunch pail, wasn't as refined or educated as Ozzie Nelson or Jim Anderson, and his wife didn't have dinner ready because she worked too. All these families had only tiny, humorous problems, and the children's misbehavior was always oh-so-cute.

In 1963 most college campuses still had strict dress codes. This wasn't always necessary because everyone expected and wanted to dress the same anyway. Most people didn't want to be different. I don't know how students dressed in other parts of the country, but in sunny Santa Barbara (UCSB) it was light blue pants (not jeans) for men, blue deck shoes, and madras shirts tucked in with a nice belt – the kind of clothes you'd see in a J.C. Penny catalogue. The women all had short, puffy hair that framed their face and pretty, modest skirts and blouses – not pants. J.C. Penny again.

Men's and women's dorms were separate, and even approved off-campus apartments in Isla Vista were separated by gender. I first lived in an apartment building divided in the middle and had a crush on Caroline, a sophomore who lived a few doors down in the women's section. One night her boyfriend was unusually loud and animated at a party, and she confided to me that he had been smoking marijuana. I'd barely heard of the stuff at the time. Somebody tried to sell me a joint outside my high school a year earlier, and I didn't even know what it was!

Leaving God
at the Isla Vista Market

I was moderately religious and very close to my church as a kid. I attended Trinity Methodist Church in Pomona regularly since first grade, sang in the choir, and was active in youth group. I was at church at least three times each week. There were also family potlucks on Fridays and Saturdays in the Fellowship Hall, and summer church camps in nearby mountains. I say "moderately" because religion didn't play much of a role in my life. I was an only child, and went to church largely to see my friends, and because my parents expected it.

My religious piety peaked the summer before college when I attended a Billy Graham rally at the L.A. Memorial Coliseum. It was awesome attending a religious event with thousands of people in the stadium where my dad took me to watch the Rams, Bruins, and Trojans play football when I was growing up, and where we watched the Dodgers play for a few years after they left Brooklyn and before Dodger Stadium opened.

Billy Graham was a powerful speaker who talked about sin and falling short, got people worried about their imperfections – possibly going to hell – and yearning for redemption. When he called us down to make a personal commitment to Jesus en masse, many people streamed down the aisles of the Coliseum, while others cheered for those going down. It was powerful moment and I was drawn down to the field to pledge whatever we pledged that day. I'm sure I meant it sincerely at the time.

So during the first months of school I still thought of myself as a religious person. I just wasn't going to church. . . week after week. But I was also learning new things in school, hearing new ideas, thinking on my own, and gradually realizing that maybe God wasn't watching after all, and maybe I didn't need religion in my life.

In March of 1964, I went to the small Methodist church in Isla Vista with my roommate Marshall, who also grew up in a Methodist church. Although we'd been living within a few blocks of the church since September, it was the first time either of us attended. We hoped there would be good refreshments at the I.V. Methodist Church, but there were none that day. We were spending all our money on booze and munchies. I don't know where we got the money for beer every day, but we had very little for food. We were disappointed and hungry as we walked home past the Isla Vista Market, so we went inside and stole some bologna, cheese and mustard, paid for a loaf of bread, then went home and made sandwiches. Church was behind me for decades after that.

Cruising and partying took a big toll on my grades that semester. When all was said and done, I was slightly below a 2.0 for the year and was asked to leave UCSB for a while. They said I could return if I went to junior college and got good grades, so after nine months of being away at a great university, I went home to my parents and my home town with my tail between my legs.

Retreat

My parents were very upset about me flunking out, of course. I enrolled in Mt. San Antonio Community College (Mt. SAC) for my second year and worked again that summer for the Pomona Park Department as a "summer casual" (student, hourly). I traveled from park to park doing whatever was needed, often with a crew of other summer workers. We spent a lot of time pulling weeds and digging ditches in the hot sun.

I made the best of a bad situation at Mt. SAC and enjoyed the classes, especially philosophy and physics, which I took only to fulfill the science requirement. In retrospect, physics and geometry were two of the most important courses I ever took because they explain much of what I see in everyday life.

In late February 1965, my philosophy professor, Dr. Thomas Hunt, came into class visibly teary-eyed and upset.

Somebody asked what was wrong and he said, "Lyndon Johnson just started bombing North Vietnam. "

I sometimes joke that half the class asked, "Where's North Vietnam?" and the other half asked, "Who's Lyndon Johnson?"

We weren't quite that dumb, but we weren't very well informed – yet. What was going on? Why was Dr. Hunt so upset?

The war in Vietnam was becoming an evening news item that year, and some people knew that the selective service (draft) was calling more and more young men for physicals and induction. Word spread that if we fell behind schedule for a four year degree (1/4 each year) we'd lose our student status, get drafted, and probably go to Vietnam. Like pieces of an ugly puzzle, our future was falling into place.

There were going away parties for friends leaving for the military, like Jack who fell behind in school and was drafted into the Army. Jack and his girlfriend got married at a going-away party in their apartment before he left for boot camp. It was a tearful event with mixed emotions. My good friend Jim enlisted in the Air Force for four years instead of getting drafted into the army for two years and almost certainly fighting in Vietnam. There was no tearful love story at Jim's party, just a few of us drinking too much and laughing. Lots of guys like Jack and Jim were leaving for the military, but we weren't yet fully aware of what that would mean.

Dr. Hunt explained the Vietnam War as best he could and then proceeded with class. Luckily, I sensed an opportunity to learn something important and decided to stay after class to find out more, which was not my habit. Over the next few weeks Dr. Hunt introduced me to a small handful of radicals and freethinkers on campus who had a different perspective on the world and knew things I didn't know and had never thought about. Very liberal politically and socially, some of them were smoking pot and trying LSD, which was legal in California until 1967, but considered very dangerous and taboo. Some people, like Dr. Timothy Leary, were doing serious research on mind expansion and philosophy. Others just enjoyed getting high and tripping.

Ironically, I attended my first "hippy" party in May 1965 while living with my square parents in my square home town, with students from a "high school with ashtrays." One young woman, tripping on acid, was a star on the school college bowl team. I saw them compete a few times and she was one of the smartest people I'd ever seen. I was surprised and impressed by her presence at this wild party, as well as by some professors who seemed comfortable in the company of stoned hippies.

This was a whole new world and I liked it!

My beliefs about many things were changing rapidly and I became convinced that the war was wrong and our leaders were lying in order to sell it to the public. I didn't yet understand much about the politics, but it made no sense to make war on third-world people in their ancestral homeland half-way around the world. Vietnam was a poor country without advanced weaponry, ICBM's, or a global Navy – how could they be a threat to us? What was really going on?

It all had to do with the Cold War, of course, and the prevailing "domino theory" which said that if one country in Southeast Asia fell to the communists, the others would fall and presumably we'd soon be surrounded. This didn't make sense to me either. Since when do countries behave like dominos?

My new friends said it was really about money and resources – mainly oil. They introduced me to books like *Silent Spring, The Power Elite, The Other America, The Rich and the Super-Rich, Labor's Untold Story, Them & Us, Who Rules America?* and *Marx and the Marxists*. I didn't read all these books, but the ideas were in the new air I was breathing. I was starting to glimpse how the system really works and I wanted to know more. I liked the people who were discussing big questions like, Is this the best we can do? Why can't we do better? What can we do about war, inequality, starvation?

I used my high school leadership skills and my position on student council to help organize and lead the first anti-war demonstration at Mt. SAC in April 1965. Although we were only about a dozen people marching around on a small junior college campus, my life was changed. I became an antiwar activist that Spring And it turns out we weren't the only small band of students marching around the colleges and universities of America. It turns out we were making a difference.

I talked to a counselor about changing my major from political science to philosophy. I only chose political science because it was the standard major for law school. Now I wanted to explore philosophy but I couldn't because I would get drafted. I was changing, but it was clear that in order to avoid the draft I had to stay in school full time, get passing grades, and stay on-track to graduate in political science in four years. After that I didn't know what would happen with the war and the draft – it seemed so distant and unreal then.

Among other things, my new friends talked about the ongoing oppression of black people and introduced me to the civil rights movement. The local CORE chapter (Congress of Racial Equality) had just completed a successful boycott of the Bank of America, pressuring the bank to increase the hiring of blacks and give them equal opportunity to succeed and advance on the job. The civil rights struggle was in the news and the racism I saw outraged me, so I was inspired to do something. I remembered the 1957 TV news coverage of federal troops escorting young black students to previously all-white schools in Little Rock, Arkansas, through mobs of hateful white people snarling vicious threats and insults. And in 1960 I watched as six-year old Ruby Bridges and her mother had to be escorted to school past hateful whites by federal marshals in New Orleans.

Flushed with pride and hope from the recent victory over BofA, the CORE meeting at a local Black church was a bit of a celebration and another amazing experience for me to witness. For one thing, I wasn't even aware of Black churches in my hometown! And I heard first-hand stories of the insults and injustices black applicants and employees endured from big, "reputable" companies. Someone announced that CORE was now turning its attention to Thriftymart, a big drug store chain (later Thrifty, then Rite-Aid) with a similar history of employment discrimination. In fact, most big companies had similar discriminatory policies and practices. CORE was helping take them down one at a time.

Compelled by a new-found passion for social justice, I found myself picketing again, this time on the east side of Garey Avenue, just south of Foothill Boulevard in my hometown of Pomona. We walked up and down the sidewalk in an oval carrying picket signs, chanting, singing, and chatting from time to time. People smiled as they passed each other, happy for the support and fellowship.

I was meeting new people, being exposed to new ideas, and having new experiences. I loved taking a stand for peace and social justice. I quickly discovered that it fed my soul. I never stopped.

In August I went back to Santa Barbara for my third year of college. As I drove west through L.A. on the Hollywood Freeway, I saw smoke rising from the Watts riots several miles to the south. Triggered by the brutal arrest of a black motorist and fueled by decades of discrimination and neglect, the rioting or rebellion – depending on your point of view – lasted six days, and resulted in 34 deaths, 1,032 injuries, 3,438 arrests, and $40 million in property damage.

I was starting to pay more attention to news events like these.

Same World, Fresh Eyes

Things were changing at UCSB and colleges across the country during school year 1965-66. One UCSB professor held a vigil against the war every Wednesday from noon to 1 p.m. at the flag pole in front of the library. He was a Quaker, so it was always a silent vigil. He was sometimes the only one standing there, but other people usually dropped by for all or part of the hour. I joined him as often as I could. Seldom more than 6-8 people, we always stood silently with no signs – nothing. I love Quakers, but I could never be one because it's hard for me to shut up. Not even a sign?

In 1965-66, psychedelic drugs swept over major colleges like a tidal wave. One of the first signs I remember was a guy sitting cross-legged in the front lawn of a beach house in Isla Vista, rubbing dirt and grass through his hair slowly and contentedly. I'd never seen such a thing before!

After my finals in early June, I hung around for a week, went to the beach and relaxed. Someone offered me some LSD and a young woman volunteered to be my "guide." It was just the two of us in her apartment, and she stayed "down" so she could help if I got confused, panicked, or needed anything. This was the protocol for taking acid the first time or two. Friends warned against tripping without someone to anchor, reassure, and help in case of a problem. And we had some thorazine which was supposed to be helpful in case of a bad trip.

There was a tall white candle on the coffee table. We sat on the couch waiting for the acid to kick in when I started seeing individual rays of light go up from the candle, bounce off the ceiling and go back down. I had never seen that before either! I think I said "Wow!" or something equally profound. I knew I was probably starting a wild ride and suddenly felt the need for a glass of water beside me.

As I walked into the kitchen I spotted a familiar yellow box of Kingsford corn starch on a shelf just below eye level. But this wasn't just another box of corn starch, it was the most beautiful and amazing box I had ever seen or ever imagined seeing. I stopped to look at the incredible design, detail, elaborate fonts, subtle colors and symmetry of the box, the way it sat squarely and proudly on the shelf. It was breathtaking! It felt like I stood there examining the box for two or three minutes, then I proceeded to the kitchen sink, filled my glass, and returned to the living room.

To my great surprise the candle was out, most of the lights were off, and my friend was curled up asleep on the couch under a blanket.

I woke her and asked what happened. "You just stood and stared at that box and I got tired, turned off some lights, and went to sleep." "How long ago was that?" She looked at her watch and said "about four hours." I've tried many times to remember or recapture something of that time with no luck.

B ut I still hadn't tried marijuana. My roommate Richard stayed in Isla Vista that summer and my girlfriend Jocelyn and I went up for a visit in August. The three of us smoked pot on the floor and watched TV. All I remember is laughing uncontrollably, and having sore face and stomach muscles the next day from the laughter. Everything was hilarious!

Those were the days when a "lid" (an ounce) was $10, a price that prevailed for many years. When the price finally rose to $15 in the 70's it was like some sacred trust had been broken – like a beloved bookkeeper embezzling from the church.

In my senior year we continued standing silently at the flag pole in front of the library each Wednesday from noon 'til 1 p.m. The anti-war movement was still relatively small and growing, but not a big deal yet. In April, 1967 the Santa Barbara antiwar community held a protest march which brought the student community together with the townies (including Quakers, progressive Jews, and Unitarians). This was part of the nationwide Mobilization to End the War in Vietnam, which was focused on the United Nations, so the largest demonstration was in New York City.

In Santa Barbara we had about 125 people marching down the sidewalk on State Street. Although small by later standards, it was the largest demonstration I had attended, and it felt great to be among a more diverse group of people, including the Wednesday-noon, flag-pole professor.

In spite of our size, I felt threatened when a handful of men emerged from a bar yelling insults and brandishing cue sticks and beer bottles. We were the peace people. What were we going to do?

Some vocal people (who, ironically, Nixon called "the silent majority") believed we were disloyal for opposing the war in Vietnam. They hated the antiwar movement, calling us traitors and "hippies." Not many of us were actually hippies at that time, but the word was used as an insult from the beginning, designed to paint the antiwar movement as self-indulgent and stoned, flighty, irrational – not to be listened to or taken seriously. This, of course, was an insult to hippies, too, because many were solid and serious people underneath the long hair and tie dye.

The anti-war people believed it was patriotic to think for ourselves and speak the truth when our country is badly off course, betraying our values, committing atrocities in our name, and damaging itself and other countries for decades to come. We remembered the warning in President Eisenhower's farewell speech:

"We must guard against the acquisition of unwarranted influence, whether sought or unsought, by the military-industrial complex. The potential for the disastrous rise of misplaced power exists and will persist. "

We didn't trust our government. The reasons it gave for the war seemed flimsy and phony.

In late 1966, notices in school and local newspapers warned of a nationwide test to be administered to those male students who wanted to stay in college. To keep our student deferments we now had to take this test and presumably get a good score. Called Selective Service Qualifying Test, it was a standardized test supposedly designed to see who was smart enough to stay in school and who was better suited for war.

Staying on track for a four-year degree was no longer enough. We now had to do well on this test.

Draft Tests To Be Given

Applications for the November 18 and 19, 1966 administrations of the College Qualification Test are now available at Selective Service System local boards throughout the country.

Eligible students who intend to take this test should apply at once to the nearest Selective Service local board for an Application Card and a Bulletin of Information for the test.

Following instructions in the Bulletin, the student should fill out his application and mail it immediately in the envelope provided to SELECTIVE SERVICE EXAMINING SECTION, Educational Testing Service, P.O. Box 988, Princeton, New Jersey 08540. Applications for the test must be postmarked no later than midnight, October 21, 1966.

According to Educational Testing Service, which prepares and administers the College Qualification Test for the Selective Service System, it will be greatly to the student's advantage to file his application at once. By registering early, he stands the best chance of being assigned to the test center he has chosen. Because of the possibility that he may be assigned to either of the testing dates, it is very important that he list a center and center number for each date on which he will be available.

Newspaper article from 1967.

Early one Saturday morning a few hundred of us at UCSB walked across the damp grass toward Campbell Hall and took a three-hour general aptitude test. Most colleges in the U.S. were like mine with young men – many with hangovers – walking across campus to take a test that might determine our future. Almost one million young men took that test in late 1966 and early 1967. Those who did poorly lost their student status and became eligible for the draft.

I did well on the test, but I'm not sure it mattered because Congress updated the Selective Service laws in early 1967, and I lost my student deferment that summer anyway when I graduated. Congress was under pressure because the war wasn't going well and was becoming increasingly unpopular. One thing people complained about was the unfairness of the draft system – who went to Vietnam and who didn't.

So just as I graduated from college and was about to enter law school they took away student deferments for many graduate students, including potential fathers. The new rules said that men who take a student deferment for graduate school would now give up their eligibility for a fatherhood deferment. Jocelyn and I were getting married later that summer and planned on having children some day, so it was a tough choice. Should I take a certain deferment (unless I flunked out again) for up to three years of law school, thereby giving up the right to a fatherhood deferment? Or should I take my chances without a

30

deferment until Jocelyn got pregnant, the draft ended, or something else happened?

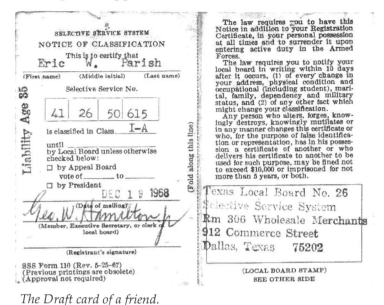

The Draft card of a friend.

— used with permission

I had been opposed to the war since 1965 and wasn't about to "participate in the immolation of Southeast Asia" as poet Steve Kowit put it. We had to make a decision by the end of the summer, and finally decided to take our chances without a student deferment. I knew I could apply for Conscientious Objector (CO) status which would keep me out for many months, maybe a year or longer. But buying time was all it would do because the selective service system was granting very few CO applications.

I would submit my own statement, of course, but it probably wouldn't convince them that I was against all wars, as CO regulations required, because I really didn't know – and I wasn't going to lie. My overwhelming feeling and motivation was that this war was unjust and I wasn't going to participate, period. Shouldn't that be enough?

Killing is murder, and should be done only when absolutely necessary. War is killing on a massive scale,

31

which should require massive justification. I saw none. Our country should be trying to evolve beyond violence as a way of settling disputes, but I saw no government attempt to do so. Our leaders were clearly going in the wrong direction. I was determined not to follow them down that path.

On the other hand, we were children of "the greatest generation" which fought and won WWII. My dad and uncles were in the service during the war and my uncles saw combat. I grew up on WWII movies and stories in which the U.S. military was always the best of the good guys. Many men in town were veterans. There was great pressure on us to go with the flow and agree that Vietnam too, was a good war, and to let the system have its way.

Life was getting complicated when I graduated from college in 1967!

Understudies

It takes time to appreciate
how we once interlaced our fingers
outside the old Fox Theater on Garey Ave,
palms out like Audie Murphy,
stretching arms in front.

Whatever happened to those simple
film gestures – the way they
loosened their helmets and smiled
to signify a lull in the fighting,
tapped a cigarette on a thumbnail
let it dangle from their lips?

Those images came with us into
the bright sunshine on the sidewalk.
We didn't yet know that just around the corner
was an office and a file with our name on it.

— Dick Eiden

The Times They Were A'changin'

War will exist until that distant day when the conscientious objector
enjoys the same reputation and prestige that the warrior does today.[1]
— JOHN F. KENNEDY

Jocelyn and I were married in a small, back-yard ceremony, and moved to Westwood after I graduated from UC Santa Barbara. I was accepted at UCLA law school and Jocelyn transferred to UCLA for her senior year as an art major. Anti-war, student power, and other liberation movements were active at UCLA and starting to make a difference throughout society. Many schools were listening to the uproar and started to admit more students who didn't fit the traditional, white male profile of law students and lawyers.

When I started in 1967 there were very few women in law school, but the 1968 entering class nationwide would jump from about five percent women to about 40 percent. Thus there were very few women in my first year class, but many more in the years to follow.

The modern feminist movement was just beginning and made a huge splash by protesting the 1968 Miss America beauty pageant for the first time. Wearing gowns with pieces of luncheon meat hanging from them, they protested "the degrading mindless-boob-girlie symbol," and our society's expectations about how women should look and act. They marched with signs, passed out pamphlets – one of them was *No More Myth America* – and mockingly crowned a live sheep as Queen in a county fair-styled livestock competition.

The student power movement was demanding that colleges and universities become less elite and traditional in students they admitted, what they taught, and how they conducted themselves.

Among other things, we wanted some democracy and transparency in governing the schools, and to be included in decisions that impacted our lives. Many liberal schools and faculties considered student demands to be reasonable and adopted them. Others just wanted to placate the students enough to avoid trouble, which was better than nothing. In either case, our faculty solicited applications and I was among the first students to serve on a faculty committee, participating in the governance of UCLA law school. But don't worry, they didn't give me any real power.

I was also one of the first to take advantage of new rules allowing law students to take up to four courses outside the law school for law school credit. The theory was that the legal profession needed lawyers to be broadly educated, interested in and knowledgeable about many things. In the spirit of the new rules, I should probably have taken a few different subjects, but I took four poetry and creative writing classes in the English Department. Poetry had always been a passion of mine.

I was also interested in philosophy. Two law school professors were well-known philosophers, so I took independent studies courses from Professors Herbert Morris and Richard Wasserstrom, and got credit for studying philosophy of laws, including *Crime and Punishment* by Fyodor Dostoyevsky, *The Genealogy of Morals* and *Thus Spoke Zarathustra* by Friedrich Nietzsche, and other such non-legal works.

In my criminal law class, Professor Ken Graham gave us a list of 10 things to choose from for our final paper. Number 10: write a poem about the relationship between Bob Dylan's *Subterranean Homesick Blues* and the criminal justice system.

That, of course, is what I did.

---

[1] Letter to a Navy friend, quoted in *A Thousand Days: John F. Kennedy in the White House,* by Arthur M. Schlesinger, Jr. (Boston: Houghton Mifflin Company, 1965), p. 88.

Civil Rights and the ACLU

I became involved with the Law Students Civil Rights Research Council (LSCRRC, pronounced *liz-crick*) in my first year and was invited to attend its law student conference in Washington, D.C., in April, 1968. I was thrilled at the chance to see the East Coast and meet activist law students from around the country.

The conference was held at Howard University, a historic black college founded in 1867 to educate newly-freed slaves. Not surprisingly, Howard stands in one of D.C.'s old, neglected, black neighborhoods.

The conference took place just a few days after Martin Luther King's assassination in Memphis. People were stunned and angry. Major riots/rebellions had occurred in Chicago, Detroit, Kansas City, Louisville, and Washington D.C. On Seventh Street and Georgia Avenue, broken glass and burned buildings provided fresh evidence of a major outpouring of grief and anger. Tensions remained high. Troops were still in the streets near the row house where I stayed.

I met lots of interesting people that week from different parts of the country and different backgrounds, all passionately interested in social justice and having fun, too. The conference had an East Coast flavor, which was new to me. I was in awe at the history, statues, monuments, and old buildings in D.C.

I received an internship from LSCRRC that summer which placed me with the Los Angeles chapter of the ACLU. I worked with a lawyer and two other law students on the recently established Police Misconduct Complaint Centers. The ACLU was involved in lawsuits from the Watts rebellion of 1965, triggered by excessive force and racial discrimination by LAPD.

Two years later, a peace march of men, women and children in Century City was brutally attacked and broken up by LAPD, without provocation.

This 1967 march was peaceful and included many educated, professional and influential "Westside liberals" – ACLU supporters among them. Elderly people and women pushing strollers were hit, knocked down. Some were arrested. They got a taste of what the black and Latino communities had experienced for decades, and what had provoked the Watts riots two years earlier. They were outraged!

When I got to the ACLU's Pershing Square offices in June 1968, the main focus was on the peace march lawsuit. The new police complaint centers were funded by a large influx of members and donations, largely thanks to the LAPD.

One center in Watts, served the black community. Another in East LA served the Latino community. One in Venice served the Westside, including Venice's black community, as well as surfers and hippies. The cops didn't seem to like surfers or hippies, either. The feeling was mutual.

We three white, middle-class law students learned a lot by spending time in the Watts and East L.A. complaint centers. These small storefronts stood in the heart of their communities. People told us horrible stories about the police and often wanted to talk about other problems with employers and landlords. Staffers helped file complaints against police when nothing else looked possible and referred the more serious cases to lawyers. They often put people in touch with community and government resources for a variety of other issues.

One morning in August, 1968 I was driving to the Watts complaint center when something seemed amiss. Listening to loud rock & roll on the two great AM stations L.A. had in those days (KRLA and KFWB), I hadn't heard the news: a small riot hit Watts the night before. Closer to the office, I began to see more police cars, then a checkpoint screening everyone entering the center of Watts. Beyond the checkpoint were some burned buildings, broken windows, and lots of glass in the street.

Our storefront office was OK, but signs of the disturbance stretched up and down Beech Street and other streets in downtown Watts. For the second time in four months, I was in the smoldering aftermath of a riot, watching people sweep glass off sidewalks.

After the summer internship I was hired by the ACLU to continue coordinating the police complaint centers, a part-time job. This mainly involved reviewing each complaint, talking to a staff lawyer, trying to find a private lawyer to talk to each person with a decent-looking case, and helping others find the resources they needed. We often helped with filing a complaint with LAPD, although we knew these would be routinely denied. We wanted to give voice to these citizens, to put pressure on the police department to reform, and to create a record of bad cops, incidents, victims, witnesses.

The Assassination of Bunchy Carter and John Huggins

In a private meeting on January 17, 1969 at UCLA's Campbell Hall – not far from the law school – leaders of the Black Panther Party (BPP) met with the rival United Slaves (US) organization. US was founded by Maulana Ndabezitha "Ron" Karenga (creator of Kwaanza) and centered in Southern California. From the law school, we could hear sirens and a commotion. I walked to Campbell Hall and found police cars and cops everywhere. That section of street had been roped off with yellow tape.

In a meeting meant to make peace, Black Panther leaders Bunchy Carter and John Huggins had been shot to death.

Several versions of what had happened made the rounds, but the murders were quickly blamed on the US organization. The animosity and trouble between the two organizations made this a logical conclusion. But like so many things in life, it turned out to be more complicated than that.

Investigations would later reveal that the FBI's Counterintelligence Program (COINTELPRO) of "dirty tricks" had been creating and fueling hostilities between the BPP and US with anonymous gossip and death threats, racist and insulting cartoons sent to one group made to look like they had been sent by the other.[1] An informant for the LAPD who infiltrated the Black movement, Louis E. Tackwood, later claimed that the federal government orchestrated the murders and had been responsible for putting the blame on various individuals, including Karenga and US (*The Glass House Tapes*: 1973)

Incredible as it seems, the FBI used the murders as a basis to raid BPP offices and apartments in L.A., arresting 75, including the remaining leaders. The charge: conspiracy to retaliate against the US organization. The pre-emptive strike fueled suspicions that the murders were part of an FBI COINTELPRO offensive to destroy the Panthers. Chicago

BPP leaders Mark Clark and Fred Hampton were shot to death in their beds in an early morning raid by Chicago police just one month earlier.

Charges against the L.A. 75 were later dropped. The murders and the raids of 1969 caused the BPP to withdraw from community outreach in order to pay more attention to security and secrecy. Disbanded in 1982, BPP would rise from the ashes more than once as racism in America continued to raise its ugly head.

The alleged shooter of Carter and Huggins escaped prosecution. Two other men went to prison for conspiracy to commit murder and second degree murder. A third man was sent to the California Youth Authority.

[1] U.S. Senate Select Committee, chaired by Senator Frank Church (D, Idaho), findings, 1975.

Fighting The Draft

I decided to stop paying taxes because taxes paid for wars. I didn't want to make it easy for them to prosecute me for tax avoidance, so in April, 1968 I wrote a letter with my earnings, deductions, and how much I owed. I indicated that I'd settle up after the war. I sent a letter like that every April until 1974 when the U.S. was finally out of Vietnam. Then, I settled up with IRS.

My last showdown with the draft took place during that second year of law school ('68-'69). My 1A draft card classification had come in the mail. I quickly applied for conscientious objector status. Although I sincerely objected to participating in the Vietnam War on grounds of conscience, there were three reasons why I knew my chances of being given CO status were slim to none.

First, the government insisted on a religious basis for believing the war was wrong. I wasn't religious any more.

Second, the draft board required an objection to all wars. I wasn't sure about that. I might have been willing to participate in a just war, but that wasn't the war I was being asked to fight.

Third, the Selective Service wasn't fair. It was serving the needs of a system that needed fresh meat. Denying CO status, even to those with impeccable credentials, helped ensure that.

Nothing was fair about this war. I knew I didn't have a chance.

Still, I filed all the paperwork and tried to make the best application I could without lying or falsifying anything. I made sure I did everything, however, at a snail's pace. I was buying time. If it was possible to delay any step of the process, I found a way. When my application was finally denied I waited until the last day to file an appeal, then dragged out the appeal process as long as possible. This strategy would serve me well in later years. By the end of 1968 I was at the end of the CO process and now had to figure out something else.

The National Lawyers Guild sponsored draft counseling at Papa Bach's Bookstore on Santa Monica Boulevard in West L.A. I went one evening amid the beads, tie-dye and incense, and talked to Peter Marx, a recent UCLA law school graduate. We reviewed my situation and quickly concluded that my only hope was some kind of medical disqualification. This would resemble the CO process, however, because the Selective Service was also very stringent on handing out medical disqualifications.

One joke about medical exemptions centered on a guy who had lost an arm and had letters and complete records from his doctors. The Selective Service doctor told him, "You have one good arm and two good legs. You pass."

Marx and others told me the L.A. induction center was among the worst in the country for medical disqualifications. We went through the medical regulations and discussed several possibilities. We shared stories about guys staying up for days at a time drinking coffee or taking no-doze to raise blood pressure, guys pretending to be gay, and even guys who shot or cut off a toe. Since there was nothing really wrong with me, I had to decide on some scheme, then roll the dice. Leaving the country was an option if all else failed, but Jocelyn and I didn't want to do that.

The height/weight chart seemed to be my only hope. Men too fat or too thin were considered unhealthy or otherwise unable to perform adequately. They would be given temporary disqualifications. I was 6' tall and weighed 145 pounds. The chart listed 131 as the lower limit for my height. So all I had to do was lose 14 pounds and transfer my physical to an induction center that might actually follow the regulations.

One day later that week, I skipped school and took an early flight to Phoenix and a taxi to Arizona State University (ASU) in nearby Tempe. I approached a young woman sitting at an anti-war table in the quad during lunchtime, explained my situation, asked if I could use her address for a few months for Selective Service purposes. She agreed to forward the mail to me, and I was on my way back to the Phoenix airport within an hour.

41

I wrote to my draft board and informed them of my new address in Arizona. Within a month or two the young lady forwarded my notice for a pre-induction physical in Phoenix in early March, 1969. I had a month to lose 10 percent of my body weight.

At first I simply cut down my portions of food, eating half as much of everything. This worked for the first two weeks. I lost a half-pound each day, right on pace to lose 15 pounds in a month. But my metabolism adjusted, so I stopped losing weight. I stopped eating entirely. For the next two weeks, I only drank water and one glass of grapefruit juice (80 calories) each day—half in the morning, half in the afternoon. My weight dropped again at a half-pound a day.

When I started this process, I had intended to continue going to school. I didn't want to drive and walk to class from remote parking lots, so I planned to take the bus from Venice to the law school and back. It was a long ride but I could sit and read. There was a bus stop on Hilgard Ave. right across from the law school, where I planned to sit quietly in the back of class and conserve my energy.

But when I stopped eating I lost all interest in or motivation for school. My head went into a completely different zone. I didn't care about the bus or school or much of anything else. I was content to sit and meditate – or whatever I was doing, mostly cross-legged on the floor.

It probably helped that I was smoking pot and/or hashish, but I don't think that made much of a difference. With or without weed I was totally spaced out. My half glass of grapefruit juice became the most important part of my day, almost sacred, as I savored every drop. At night I dreamed about hamburgers, especially L.A.s famous Tommy Burgers, oozing chili. But mainly those two weeks passed in peaceful meditation and listening to rock & roll. It was a surprisingly wonderful spiritual experience.

When the time came I was pretty confident I'd weigh in at 130 pounds or less. I didn't think 130 was good enough, however. They might say, as they would in L.A., "close enough, we'll fatten you up - you pass." I was too spaced out to drive, so Jocelyn drove all six hours across the desert to Phoenix. We got a room in a cheap motel near the induction center downtown, in the bus station district. On the morning of the physical I took a diuretic to minimize my water content, and I spat as much as I could into my handkerchief. Short of shooting off my big toe or openly having sex with a radical priest, I had done pretty much everything I could to be disqualified for killing.

I was weak, of course, and felt faint while standing in one line after another all morning, but I tried not to let on. As far as they were concerned, this had to be my normal weight. I stood as tall and straight as I could when they measured my height and made sure they recorded it correctly. It needed to say 6', and that's what he wrote. Then I watched the scale carefully and made sure they recorded the number correctly – 128. *Yippee*!

I was still worried they might classify me 1A, but knew I had grounds for an appeal if they did. An appeal might buy me another year, so I was happy enough at the numbers on the paper.

A few weeks later the ASU student forwarded another letter from the Selective Service which said I was classified 3Y: temporarily disqualified for medical reasons. This was the best I could expect. They didn't give 4F permanent disqualifications for a few pounds underweight. I'd have to flunk three times and take my next physical in six months, but I had a leg up, skinny as it was. I established grounds for a medical disqualification. All I had to do was keep my weight down and fail two more tests.

My tastes in food changed considerably after fasting for a month. I was more in touch with my body than before, and all I wanted was simple, unrefined foods without spices, sugar or grease. It took several weeks to become conditioned to eating regular American food again. I wish I hadn't gone back. I enjoyed the simple foods, but society makes it hard to stay on that path, and after a while I stopped trying. Within a few months I was back to my old eating habits. Of course, I still watched my weight.

Because I was now a *3Y retest*, I thought I could flunk the physical even in L.A., so I changed my residence back. In August I didn't have to drive to Phoenix or go through the whole physical again. For the retest I was just measured and weighed and sent on my way. I failed the retest in August, then continued to keep my weight down. I expected to take another retest in the winter.

Two things intervened to keep me from taking that third test. First, the national draft lottery debuted on December 1, 1969. Politicians were getting pressure to change the draft system, which almost everyone hated. For one thing, there was a lot of uncertainty about who would serve. "Certainty" was why they supposedly gave the 1966-67 aptitude test for students, which hadn't quelled the unrest or eased the pressure on politicians. So a lottery was invented.

Numbers representing each day of the year were printed on blue plastic balls in a large glass container. The lottery would apply to every man born between January 1, 1944 and December 31, 1950. The lowest numbers drawn would be subject to the draft. The higher numbers would be free to make other plans, school or not.

The first ball was drawn in a televised ceremony by Congressman Alexander Pirnie of the House Armed Services Committee. Officials predicted that everyone above the middle (about 182) would be free. My birthday – May 22 – pulled number 326. I was finally out of it. Completely. Forever.

About this time, we found out Jocelyn was pregnant. Because I hadn't taken a student deferment for law school, I was now eligible for a fatherhood deferment as well. After almost three years of battle, I suddenly had three ways to a permanent deferment, and a precious baby on the way.

The Draft Lottery Begins
December 1, 1969

LAPD Attack at UCLA

My law school career ended with a bang, not a whimper. One sunny day in May, 1970, I took my lunch to Janss Steps – 87 steps in a wide brick staircase up a grassy hillside, and the original entrance to UCLA. The top of Janss Steps opens to a quad between the main library and Royce Hall, two of the oldest and most central buildings on campus. I sat on the grass near the top of the hill looking down on the men's and women's gyms below, and at scores of other people eating lunch on the grass that beautiful day.

A small group of antiwar demonstrators was picketing in front of the men's gym, which housed ROTC (reserve Officers' Training Corps) – a source of controversy and the target of protests on many campuses. President Nixon had just announced the invasion of Cambodia. Protests were taking place around the country. The anti-war movement felt the military had no business recruiting and training on campus and that schools had no business training students to be part of a war machine and the *do what you're told* military mentality. Students wrote letters to the editor and protested. Most didn't care that much that Spring day. They were just having lunch and walking here and there on campus. Some of us cared. I had protested ROTC at other times, but couldn't attend every protest. This lunchtime was simply lunchtime for me, too.

I didn't think much about it when some of the demonstrators threw rocks that broke a small window in the men's gym at the bottom of the hill. Most of us continued talking and eating lunch on the grass.

Janss Steps face west, from which direction I heard a dull roar. As I looked to see what it was, a long line of police motorcycles began to emerge from around a hill on Sunset Boulevard. All of us on the hill were watching now.

The seemingly endless line of motorcycles snaked around the corner two by two. The roar got louder. It seemed as if 100 motorcycles or more had entered the campus and filed into a parking lot directly in front of us, just beyond the two gyms and a small internal street. I wondered how that many cops appeared so quickly, because the group was peaceful except the broken windows, which happened just a few minutes earlier. Were they expecting trouble? Did they know someone would create an excuse to attack

The protesters finally quieted down and turned to watch what the police would do. At first they didn't hear the roar of engines because of their own noise. Their down-the-hill position blocked their view of what we were seeing from atop the steps

Janss Steps, UCLA

photograph by the author

The police dismounted, parked their bikes, put on their gear – helmets and batons – then got into formation and marched east toward the gyms, the demonstrators, and, as it turned out, all of us eating lunch.

At the front of the gym, the police started grabbing everybody in sight. Maybe they couldn't distinguish the demonstrators from the passers-by. The demonstrators and spectators ran in all directions, chased by a small group of police. The main body of police kept moving east toward us! *What the hell?*

An English professor sharing lunch with a group of students near the bottom of the steps was grabbed. So were others nearby. The police kept coming up the hill. When the rest of us realized what this unexpected development meant, we began to scatter. Being near the top, I ran east across the quad toward the law school and administration building. A mass of helmeted, baton-swinging cops followed us.

Although tempted to keep running and leave the campus as the police were ordering us to do, many stayed to see what would happen. Students were pissed off and started fighting back in the only ways they knew. As individuals and small groups, we played catch-me-if-you-can with LAPD. We knew the campus better than they did. Small groups of students threw rocks from the roofs of buildings, then disappeared before the police could mount an attack. Students then regrouped on another roof or somewhere else.

The cops assumed that anyone left in the area was a rock-thrower or other law breaker, so they chased everyone they saw. At one point a cop spotted me and started chasing. I ducked into the nearby English building where I had taken classes. He followed me down halls and up stairs and was still behind me when I rounded a corner and ran into a dead end. Trapped, I turned and raised my hands. I remember thinking, "You've got me. What are you going to do now?"

We were alone in that hallway, maybe in the whole building. The police officer slowed down, stopped a few feet in front of me, paused, then turned and walked away. He hadn't seen me do anything illegal. Why would he arrest me? Still, that hadn't stopped other cops from making arrests that day. I knew I was very lucky. After several hours, things died down. Most everyone had gone home.

As bad as things were at UCLA, May 4th would be remembered as the day four students were shot and killed by National Guard troops at Kent State University in Ohio. Eleven days later, two students were killed and 12 were injured when police opened fire on an anti-war protest at Jackson State, a historically black university in Mississippi. The war had come home.

Our son Demian, born later that month, was 17 days old when we took him out in public for the first time. Law School graduation was held outdoors on the quad near the top of Janss Steps, where six weeks earlier, I had made my first run from the police.

It would not be my last.

II

MOVING INTO THE MOVEMENT

Cautious, careful people, always casting about to preserve their reputation and social standing, never can bring about reform. Those who are really in earnest must be willing to be anything or nothing in the world's estimation, and publicly and privately, in season or out, avow their sympathy with despised and persecuted ideas and their advocates, and bear the consequences.

—*SUSAN B. ANTHONY*

The Interview

One day *The Daily Bruin* ran a notice about a lawyer giving a talk to the UCLA Democratic Club about Selective Service law. After all I'd been through to get out of the draft, I considered myself a minor expert on medical deferments and wanted to hear what he had to say. The law school at UCLA was near the center of the main campus, where there were meetings, speeches and activities of every kind each week – more than I could possibly keep up with.

This meeting would be in the philosophy building, next to the law school. The speaker turned out to be a hip young guy with a solo practice in Hollywood, specializing in draft cases. Mike Grodsky didn't look like Perry Mason. He wasn't wearing a suit and tie. He had a thick, drooping mustache, shoulder-length hair and acted brash and irreverent, not conservative and cautious. He spoke frankly about the terrible war, the draft, the government. It was all very refreshing!

I spoke with him after his talk, told him I was finishing law school, and about my experience with the draft. He said he'd been a lawyer for three years, just long enough to get some clients and team up with another attorney in renting a ground floor office in Hollywood, hiring a secretary and receptionist. He now had enough business that he was interested in hiring and training a new lawyer. He invited me to call him when I passed the bar exam, which would hopefully be in a few months. Jocelyn and I were expecting our son so I was very excited about the possibility of a paying job using my hard-won legal knowledge to do something helpful for others, including the Vietnamese, who didn't need any more young Americans over there making war on them.

Demian was six months old in early December when I learned I had passed the bar exam and would be admitted in a ceremony on January 7, 1971. I called Mike to see if he was still interested in talking and he invited Jocelyn and me to his home in Hollywood to discuss the job. After meeting his wife and exchanging some pleasantries they invited us, as was the custom in those days, to smoke some pot. He described it as "amazing weed." I think he was right, but it was hard for me to tell.

My cat allergies kicked in with a vengeance about the time we were passing the first joint around. Within 10 minutes of entering my prospective employer's home, I was so stoned, my head so stuffed up, and my eyes watering so badly I could hardly see or think. After trying to act normally for a few minutes I jumped up from the low couch, desperate to find the bathroom and splash water on my eyes and face. But I could barely navigate to the bathroom past the coffee table, tea pot, candles, incense burner, legs and feet, a straw basket, the turned-over corner of a rug, and the cats. I stumbled to the bathroom as if in the aisle of an airplane in heavy turbulence, hands held out for whatever wall, seat back or other solid object I could find. I may have fallen, I'm not sure, I was in a thick haze.

My head was still stuffy and my eyes watering when I returned to the living room couch, but my panic was now under control. Aware of having embarrassed myself, I was fairly confident that I could breathe without gasping, regain composure, and perhaps redeem myself. Mike didn't seem bothered by my behavior at all. He acted as though he had half-expected such a response to such amazing weed. He probably took it as a compliment. I tried to explain that I can usually handle good weed, but the long haired cats had put me over the edge. I told my stupid story about how I discovered my cat allergy while studying for an economics exam one Spring in Isla Vista.

Mike was very agreeable, and quite stoned himself. He was excited to show me "a new toy" he had recently purchased. Smiling, I kept concentrating on my breathing as he returned cradling a large .45 caliber automatic on a white rag. Through my haze, I could see he was inviting me to hold it.

I felt strongly that weapons and warrior-worship were part of a dangerous national illness inherited from our primitive past. Made only to kill and injure others, handguns were a symbol of man's inhumanity to man. And in my condition, this gun looked like the largest, heaviest, hardest piece of dark metal I had ever seen.

Still, I tried to be agreeable, held the gun for a moment, smiled and nodded approvingly as I passed it back to him. I thought, it's not always necessary to fall on a sword over principle. Presumably I would have other chances to talk to Mike about issues. He was against the war, doing something about it, and offering me a job. That was good enough for one night.

A Career Born in the Politics of War

On January 7, 1971, hundreds of new State Bar admittees formed a line in the quad between the L.A. County Hall of Administration and the Civil Courthouse. We were about to walk across Grand Street to the Dorothy Chandler Pavilion where our families waited for the swearing-in ceremony to begin.

Young people from the National Lawyers Guild – including some activists who had graduated in the class ahead of mine at UCLA – handed out leaflets urging us to protest the war by raising our fist instead of our open hand when being sworn in. That sounded good to me – a quiet but powerful statement against the war.

A state judge swore us into the California courts first. About 200 of us quietly raised our right fist instead of our open hand. Then a grumpy old guy from the federal bench came up to swear us in to the U.S. District Court, but instead of swearing us in he said he was outraged by our behavior which he called unpatriotic, disrespectful and unprofessional. He said he wouldn't swear anybody in that day, that in order to get sworn in to the federal district court we'd have to go to the clerk's office and first take an oath that we were not among those who raised our fist during the ceremony Only then would anyone be sworn in.

Most everyone – including those who didn't raise fists– thought he was being outrageous. Was taking a false oath any way to start a law career? Almost everyone refused to go down and be sworn in. Memories of loyalty oaths and McCarthyism still hung in our collective consciousness. Whatever our stand on the war, we had been through law school together, passed the bar together, and we had all earned the right to practice law, godammit!

A standoff lasted about two weeks. Only those people who had jobs or needed to be sworn in to federal court, or those who supported the war and agreed with the judge went down to take the oath. We got news of developments from *The Daily Journal*, L.A.'s legal newspaper, and from the law schools. This incident received lots of attention locally, which defeated the judge's purpose of silencing dissent.

Reports cited judges, law school deans and others urging the federal judges to give in. Some didn't agree with the presiding judge anyway. Others felt he had gone too far or that the point had been made.

The solidarity of many who didn't raise their fists proved vital. After some two weeks of negotiation, the federal court relented and dropped the additional oath. I went to the clerk's office and was sworn in within days.

Draft Lawyers in Hollywood

Mike's office was at 6600 Sunset Boulevard next to Zig Zag Bail Bonds. Business was good. The draft was going strong. Young people were coming from all over the country to get arrested for drugs and prostitution in Hollywood. Mike was high on the life of a young, hip Hollywood lawyer, and was determined to enjoy himself. First he purchased a strange red, white, and blue striped muscle car with a scoop on the hood, raised in front with oversized wide tires in back. It was a race car, but he just drove it to work, the airport, and around town. The strangest thing was that it was made by American Motors, the same company that made the Nash Metropolitan and the Rambler – the opposite of muscle cars.

Then Mike got a pilot's license and bought a small airplane. Like many young lawyers, he loved the image of being busy and important. Owning expensive toys signified that. Scheduled to give a talk on draft law to the Democratic Club at Long Beach State, Mike chose to drive his muscle car to the Van Nuys Airport, then fly to Long Beach, where a small entourage of students would pick him up. Our office stood halfway between Van Nuys and Long Beach. He could have driven to Long Beach in the time it took him to get to his plane!

Most of Mike's talks were given to groups like the campus Democratic Clubs – anti-war and anti-draft, full of potential clients, and friends of potential clients. These trips built the practice, but they also bolstered Mike's ego. There was a special spring to his step, a sparkle in his eyes as he bounded out of his plane and extended a hand to students greeting him. The image he created was of an important guy with an important message – "I can save your ass for a mere 350 bucks."

It would have been unwise and unethical to guarantee results, but Mike came close. He talked about his great track record of keeping people out of the draft. He added a wink, suggesting he had a big secret. And he did. I thought Mike might have been the kind of guy who would make promises he couldn't keep if he had to, but in this case, he didn't have to.

There were two aspects to our Selective Service practice. On one hand, we stayed on top of the law by attending meetings and seminars, subscribing to relevant publications, and being part of a network of lawyers who shared information. We also learned a lot in handling our cases. The goal in every case was to find a legal loophole in the laws or their administration that might delay the process and get the client out of the draft. Led by Los Angeles National Lawyers Guild lawyer and organizer William G. "Bill" Smith, lawyers found creative ways to attack the bureaucracy of the Selective Service System with great success. Letters, phone calls, documents, appeals – lots of paperwork, lots of delay. We preferred this approach. The work justified our fee, and it was all above board.

In those few cases where that approach failed, we got down and dirty – *guerrilla law*. Clients called for induction physicals were advised of the medical regulations in great detail. Blood pressure was of special interest. A person can temporarily raise their blood pressure just by flexing the sphincter muscle. We never advised them to do such a thing – that would be unethical. Most of our clients managed to have high blood pressure and fail their physicals without doing any damage to themselves. If some other alternative might work, we would jump on it. Blood pressure was a last resort.

In those years I had four clients who called me from the induction center saying the doctor was concerned because their blood pressure was dangerously high. The doctor wanted to have each taken to a hospital immediately. The first time I got this call I was surprised. "Thank the doctor for his concern, " I said, thinking on my feet. "And tell him you'll go home and make an appointment with your own doctor right away." I trust that's what they all did.

Mike and I attended monthly meetings of the draft law panel. Bill Smith came to each meeting with a pile of articles, newsletters, regulations, letters, and news of developments in draft law regulations and cases, as well as information he heard from other lawyers who called him frequently with questions and information. Lawyers from all over the country knew that Bill Smith was the guy to call.

After one panel meeting, I talked to a lawyer whose office represented Geronimo Pratt, a leader of the Black Panther Party (BPP), then in the Hall of Justice Jail (HOJJ) awaiting trial on murder and kidnapping charges. The NLG got involved because evidence surfaced that Pratt did not commit the crime. With the government's history of attacks on BPP leaders, Geronimo Pratt might be being framed. That suspicion proved right!

Pratt was the target of a COINTELPRO operation designed to "neutralize him as an effective Black Panther Party functionary."[1] His conviction was vacated and he was released in 1997 after 27 years in prison, eight in solitary confinement.

Black Panther leaders wanted to talk to "Gee" about the case against him and about BPP business, but there was no hope of a private conversation in the normal visiting areas. His lawyers added my name to their legal team and I was able to take these visitors to meet with him in the attorney area, which afforded more privacy. Even a new lawyer who didn't know much could help.

I took Kathleen Cleaver to see Gee a few times. In addition to being Eldridge Cleaver's wife, she was a BPP leader in her own right. Beautiful, radical, big Afro and very well known, she attracted a lot of attention wherever she went. The jail deputies didn't like her – or anyone with her. Once while being patted-down during the jail entry procedure, a deputy ran his hands over my pantlegs, bringing one hand up into my balls very hard, presumably to indicate he didn't like me or what I was doing.

HOJJ housed several well-known people at that time. Charles Manson's trial had recently ended and I often saw him meeting with his lawyers in the attorney room. Because he was still being held at HOJJ, the "Manson girls" still sat all day in a tight circle on the sidewalk at Temple and Broadway, those crude carvings in their foreheads. The Manson clan was shrouded in devilish mystery. When one of the Manson attorneys, Ron Hughes, was found dead on a short camping trip during the trial, speculation arose about how he had died.

Security at HOJJ was very high at all times, but especially when Charlie Manson and Geronimo Pratt were in the attorney visiting area at the same time.

I spoke with Gee through a rectangular opening in a concrete block wall which had two layers of thick wire mesh about two inches apart between us. Strangely, it's completely different than looking through one layer of mesh. With only one layer, the eye and brain can ignore the wire and focus on the person. But staring through two layers of wire mesh always made me dizzy and nauseated.

Luckily, I didn't have to get dizzy very often because my presence in the conversations wasn't needed or desired. I was just a prop. Kathleen may have been a witness to some aspect of this case or another, but I guessed she wasn't talking about the case. Neither she nor Gee wanted me to hear what they were discussing. That was fine with me. I sat as far from them as possible while maintaining the awkward illusion that this was an attorney conference with a witness.

---

[1] *New York Times*, June 3, 2011, and the partially redacted COINTELPRO file on Geronimo Pratt.

Santa Barbara Legal Collective

During this time I visited my alma mater and met some student activists and NLG lawyers. UC-Santa Barbara became a hotbed of antiwar protests and a vanguard of the emerging counter-culture movement after I left for law school four years earlier. UCSB students – allegedly led by Associated Student Body (ASB) Vice President Greg Knell – marched onto the runway and shut down the Santa Barbara airport for hours during one protest.

An Isla Vista anti-war protest erupted in rioting for several days in April, 1970. Among other things, the local Bank of America caught fire while being trashed, and it burned to the ground. A student, Kevin Moran, was shot to death while trying to put out the fire. The Santa Barbara Sheriff's department immediately claimed Moran was shot by a radical sniper, even issued an All Points Bulletin, complete with a description of the get-away car. It would later be revealed that Moran was killed by a local police officer, allegedly an accident.

The first half of June 1970 saw 667 arrests in and around Isla Vista during protests against both ROTC and against increasingly heavy-handed police tactics and brutality. It was later determined that the Santa Barbara Sheriff's Department overreacted to the protests and ran amok during those weeks. Even conservative commentator William F. Buckley criticized the Santa Barbara Sheriff's Department response to the riots as "utterly senseless examples of repression."[1]

As part of running amok and looking for scapegoats, the county charged 17 campus and off-campus radicals and anti-war leaders with conspiracy to riot and arson. That group included ASB Vice President Greg Knell. Local lawyers joined the defendants to conduct a defense as a collective team of intelligent political people. This reflected a leftist trend that valued each person equally – lawyer or not – and expected each defendant to stay informed, to contribute to the defense, and to be heard.

This was quite contrary to the normal lawyer-client relationship in which the lawyer acts as the expert and decides everything about legal issues and strategy.

The lawyers in this 1970 case believed that smart defendants could learn everything they needed to know in order to participate fully in discussions and decisions about their case. And they did. Most of the defendants were acquitted of all charges. One was convicted and went to prison. Two jumped bail and went underground – not uncommon in those days.

Lawyers, defendants and student volunteers formed strong bonds during the pre-trial months and the 16-week trial. They discussed starting a law office – a legal collective. I knew some of them. We began talking after the trial in the Spring of 1971. Informal discussions turned into formal meetings through that summer. By October, I was back in town and part of the Santa Barbara Legal Collective.

Four lawyers, six legal workers, and a few large dogs opened our office. Three of the legal workers were defendants in the conspiracy trial. The other three lawyers represented them. I became the resident draft lawyer.

That summer, the National Lawyers Guild held its annual convention in Boulder, Colorado. There was a struggle going on within the NLG which mirrored a larger political struggle between the "new left" and the "old left." As law students, the new left inside the NLG had made its first assault on the old order at its 1968 convention in Washington, D.C. Many old- left lawyers had become established and displayed the trappings of successful attorneys. Some were among those who formed the NLG back in 1937, when the American Bar Association refused to admit black lawyers as members.

These older, pioneering lawyers were rightfully proud of the organization they had built, and of its work during and after WWII. Los Angeles lawyers Ben Margolis, John McTernan and A.L. Wirin served on the front lines representing unions in the '30's, immigrant workers in the '40s, the Civil Rights movement, the Hollywood Ten and other writers and movie professionals who had been blacklisted, persecuted, and prosecuted during the Cold War for their leftist beliefs, activities, and even their friendships.

These older NLG lawyers clashed with my '60s generation at the 1968 convention. Like most conventions, the traditional dinner offered a pricey meal in a banquet room of an upscale hotel. The new lefties, still in law school, felt disenfranchised. Welcome at the convention, law students were not full members of the NLG and therefore could not vote. Most didn't have fancy clothes or enough money for the banquet. Broke, and wearing nontraditional clothing, they crashed the 1968 NLG convention banquet and served notice that change was in the air – and in the room.

The NLG poised for another showdown as the 1971 convention approached. Those same law students from 1968 were now lawyers. The new left and the youth culture had grown both inside and outside the NLG. Women and students would no longer be easily marginalized or disenfranchised. The era of banquet halls with male, cigar-smoking leftist lawyers in suits and ties was now quickly coming to an end.

Most of this historical significance was lost on our nascent collective in Santa Barbara. We were simply going to the convention as we were – California hippie lawyers. Some in our group were devoted to dogs named Che, Fidel, and Trotsky, who they wouldn't dream of leaving behind. We piled as many people and dogs as possible into Alan Schlosser's blue Ford Econoline van, then cranked the stereo as high as it would go. Trailing a cloud of marijuana smoke, we drove east, toward a showdown we knew nothing about.

We were not the only young radicals drawn to this convention. Poor, young Movement lawyers and law students converged on the University of Colorado from every part of the country. To keep expenses down, we rented as few dorm rooms as possible, crowding in as many people and dogs as we could. Without trying, we had completely overwhelmed the old guard of the NLG and the university staff. Dorm hallways were littered with sleeping bags. We openly smoked pot, cooked on hot plates in rooms and hallways. The dorm staff couldn't keep up.

61

Delegates clashed in meetings. The new left took organizational control of the NLG, for better or worse. By-Laws were changed to allow law students and "prison lawyers" to join as voting members. The "banquet" would become an inexpensive dinner – spaghetti, salad and bread that year. Suits and ties would no longer be required or particularly desired at any function. Depending on one's point of view, this was either anarchy or chaos, or a very groovy happening.

I rode home from Denver with two law students – Barbara Honig and Gary Silbiger – and a recent law school grad, Steve Hollopeter, whom I first met at UCSB frosh camp in 1963. These three would become my closest friends and associates a few years later.

On the long drive to L.A., Steve introduced us to "the little red book"– *Quotations from Chairman Mao Tse-Tung*. We discussed Mao's ideas while sharing thoughts about the convention, the NLG, The Movement, the war, and the world.

Meeting great new people, feeling part of a movement, winning organizational struggles, and deepening ties with my new Santa Barbara associates, I felt like I'd found leftist hippy heaven.

The egalitarian nature of our legal collective required our names be listed in alphabetical order. Though the youngest and greenest lawyer, my name came first: Eiden, Imhoff, Schlosser & Solomon. Our letterhead listed 10 names, also in alphabetical order. Only four had "lawyer" following their names. We would later be reported to the State Bar Association and disciplined for listing non-lawyers on our letterhead. Egalitarianism evidently offended the State Bar. We were ordered to remove the non-lawyer names from our letterhead. We were also ordered to stop calling ourselves "Santa Barbara Legal Collective" in legal matters. We complied of course, but, being poor and frugal, we felt compelled to use up our supply of old stationary first.

It's hard for me to imagine a precedent for the Santa Barbara Legal Collective. There were other political collectives emerging throughout the country, but we existed in the counter-culture heaven of a Southern California beach town. We rented space downtown – no fancy carpeting, no walls made-to-order, no big expenses. We painted and cleaned up before we hauled in our rag-tag collection of used and unmatched furniture. However humble, it had a warm and cozy feel – an unpretentious place set up for hard work and good intentions.

We opened a satellite office in Isla Vista, more like a flop-house for homeless hippies and stray dogs than anything else. We called it the "Isla Vista Department of Justice" to mock the government and the system. The DJ, as we called it, fit the down and out mood of Isla Vista in those days. Sex, drugs, rock, roll, and the riots attracted people on the weird edge of radicalism, poverty, addiction, and cultural craziness. Little remained of the innocent "summer of love" idealism of 1967 when I last lived there. That sentiment was still there, but harder to find under new layers of crud and cynicism.

During weekly meetings, we discussed each case, as well as the other business of the collective. Democracy reigned over efficiency. The meetings ran long, but we all learned and bonded during the process. We also held political education meetings to study political economy, leftist philosophers, and prison books like *Soul on Ice* by Eldridge Cleaver and *Soledad Brother: The Prison Letters of George Jackson*.

We worried about opening an office and supporting 10 people, but things began to work out. For one thing, many radical and counter-culture people with legal problems started coming to us right away. They were glad to see an office like ours, thumbing our noses at the system while working within it. Hippies and counter-culture folks worked hard at art, crafts, and small businesses. We wanted to support people like them. There was a new free clinic in town, only the second in California, plus a food co-op, also a radical concept in the age of supermarkets.

The most important reason we attracted clients was because my colleagues – lawyers and non-lawyers alike – were well known and respected due to the long, well-publicized conspiracy trial that had dominated the local news for months. Each of the other lawyers had experience and credentials that inspired confidence. I, on the other hand, had little experience, but knew draft law. That proved important to our financial survival and to our opposition to the war. The draft was still going strong. I attracted clients and brought in more than my share of income to the office – even though my standard fee was only $35. That was 10% of what Mike and I had charged in L.A. This legal collective had no muscle cars or airplanes to support, but I still wondered if I should have charged more. We all lived in poverty at first.

During my two years in the legal collective, we spent many afternoons picketing the local Safeway in support of the grape strike by Caesar Chavez and the United Farm Workers. For months on end, we closed the office at 4 p.m. each Thursday to cross the street and picket as a group. We also joined the Alternative Businessperson's Association in order to support untraditional businesses and grow our own firm. We were trying to figure out how to use our skills and consciousness to make a difference, to help change the world. Besides trying to end the war and injustice, we were trying to build a new, self-sustaining counter-culture.

We still had bills to pay. There was too little money for 10 people and their dogs. I lived in a large room in a very old Victorian house, often counting my change at the end of the day to see if I could afford a beer or two. Others went dumpster-diving for food.

But even when I had next to no money, I enjoyed some wonderful Happy Hours at restaurants and bars on State Street. I could usually get someone to join me. One Mexican restaurant had a full selection of free food during weekday Happy Hour – bowls of guacamole and chips, shrimp cocktail, nachos. Other places had reduced prices and beautiful patios. And every place served great margaritas.

A popular young activist who had lived in Santa Barbara all his life planned to run for a seat on the City Council. No Latino had ever won a seat for that local public office, and strict regulations appeared to guarantee that this young activist would not be permitted to run. Leo Martinez lived outside the city limits for a short time two years earlier. Santa Barbara required continuous residence for five years before any election.

Enter a promising young woman who had recently joined us as a paralegal. Joanne Frankfurt came with no legal training or experience. She was a serious and intelligent student, with solid politics. Guided by Richard Solomon, our most experienced lawyer, Joanne did all the basic research and wrote the first draft of our pleadings. An original writ was filed with the California Supreme Court–a highly uncommon procedure, designed for quick results.

The writ was granted almost immediately. The state Supreme Court held that a four-year residency requirement was unreasonable, and ordered Leo Martinez to be placed on the ballot.[2] Martinez won that election. He would serve four years on the Santa Barbara City Council.

A legal and political grand slam had been hit by someone with no formal legal training. Take that, you sexist, elitist, racist, capitalist snobs!

[1] *New York Times*, August 30, 1970.

[2] Supreme Court of California, In Bank: January 30, 1973.

65

VVAW
and the 1972 GOP Convention

The pioneers of a warless world are the youth
who refuse military service. —ALBERT EINSTEIN

In early 1972, the Santa Barbara Legal Collective was asked to host a meeting to plan anti-war demonstrations at the Republican National convention in August. The Republicans had chosen San Diego as the site, presumably to nominate an increasingly unpopular President Nixon. The Southern California antiwar movement was delighted to have this important event in our back yard. The last round of conventions in 1968 had produced an outpouring of rage at the war and the corrupt politics which President Lyndon Johnson and Chicago Mayor Richard Daley represented. That same war was still going strong. The antiwar movement had grown. Vietnam Veterans Against the War (VVAW) had emerged as a powerful voice. Everyone expected a large, loud, and spirited demonstration in San Diego that August.

Anti-war leaders in L.A. looked for a weekend retreat out of town to plan their convention activities, so they invited themselves up to Santa Barbara. We were honored to accept. Among the participants were Jane Fonda, her husband, Tom Hayden, and their son Troy, a toddler. Sitting on floors and eating seeds, nuts and sprouts, we had excellent, mellow meetings, and good times. We made plans. Although I spent much of my time running errands to facilitate the meetings, I got to meet a host of talented people and learned how to organize major events.

On May 5th, the GOP changed its plans, suddenly moving the convention to Miami. This unusual last-minute move, just three months before a national convention, upset plans that had been made, contracts signed, and money exchanged years in advance. The change was officially blamed on labor and cost concerns in San Diego, but that appeared to be an obvious lie.

Rumors of a bribe circulated. International Telephone and Telegraph (ITT) allegedly paid $400,000 to the GOP – as a "donation" – to hold the convention in San Diego, in exchange for the Nixon Justice Department dropping an antitrust case. The allegation turned out to be true.

There was good reason to believe the sudden change was partly because San Diego would draw a large, angry and organized protest from all over Southern California and beyond. Yippee! (Youth International Party) leaders Abbie Hoffman and Jerry Rubin claimed they would bring a million protesters to San Diego, which Nixon had labeled his "lucky city," always delivering votes to him. More realistic estimates calculated 100,000 to 200,000 people might descend on the convention. That amounted to 20 times the number that showed up in Chicago four years earlier. Neither the GOP nor San Diego civic leaders wanted a chaotic protest like that 1968 convention, when 23,000 police and national guard clashed with 10,000 protestors in front of the International Ampitheater and throughout downtown – all captured on the national news.

Nixon's order to mine Haiphong harbor and other North Vietnamese ports in early May set off protests, rioting, and confrontations on campuses around the country. Protests and battles in Isla Vista took place all month between young people in tie-dyed clothes and Santa Barbara Sheriff Deputies in riot gear. Holding formation, Deputies shot tear gas at us. Activists threw rocks in return. Some brave souls with bandanna masks and improvised gloves tossed tear gas canisters back at the police.

By 1972, Isla Vista had become a focal point for antiwar unrest. Fighting with law enforcement each spring was now standard operating procedure. A friend of mine, Geoff, had lived in Isla Vista for years. He was used to the new dynamic. When we got tired of running through the streets half blinded by tear gas, we went to his apartment and snorted lines of coke, his drug of choice, then rejoined the joyful chaos with renewed energy.

Lenin referred to rebellions and revolutions as "festivals of the oppressed." Indeed!

Caravan to Miami

That Spring my marriage began falling apart. I started dating Jeannie, a student activist at UCSB who was graduating and headed to law school. We heard that VVAW was organizing car caravans to the GOP convention in Miami, and we decided to go with them. Formed in 1967 by six veterans who attended an anti-war march in New York City, VVAW rose to prominence with the 1971 Winter Soldier Investigations, which heard public testimony from veterans who witnessed war crimes by our own military. Armed with that testimony, VVAW organized operation Dewey Canyon III, named after two illegal military invasions of Laos by U.S. and South Vietnamese forces. Referred to as a "Limited incursion into the country of Congress *Land*"[1] (mocking the Nixon administration's defense of the invasions which had been prohibited by Congress), hundreds of veterans converged on Washington D.C. for a week in April, camped out on the National Mall, met with members of Congress, attended congressional and public meetings, and spoke at churches and organizations about what was really happening in Vietnam.

The high point of the week came on April 22, when hundreds of Vietnam Veterans threw thousands of their medals – bronze stars, silver stars, purple hearts, even Honorable Discharge papers – onto the steps of the Capitol. Condeming comments filled the air: "If we have to fight again, it will be to take these steps."

The government feared demonstrations by angry veterans with military training and experience. A chain-link fence was erected around the Capitol building. Documentaries and video clips show young veterans walking, limping, being wheeled, and throwing their medals over that fence onto the white marble steps. Many vets made short, moving statements. One made a memorable statement: U.S. Navy Lt. John Kerry would later become a Senator from Massachusetts, the Democratic candidate for President in 2004, and Secretary of State in the Obama administration in 2013.

VVAW organized to protest at each party nominating convention. Both were now being staged in Miami. In May, eight members of the Gainsville VVAW were arrested and indicted for conspiracy to use weapons and disrupt the Democrat convention. The Gainsville Eight sat in a Tallahassee jail awaiting trial.

In that summer of 1972, VVAW found itself in the government's crosshairs when it organized three car caravans to converge on Miami and the GOP convention in August. Called The Last Patrol, one caravan would leave from Cal State Northridge, in L.A.'s San Fernando Valley. Another caravan left from Boston. The third hailed from Minneapolis.

We drove south from L.A. to San Diego, then east across the southern part of the country to Jacksonville, then south to Miami. Traveling convoy style, in single file, lights on, 55 mph, in the right lane, we started with 10 cars. We picked up VVAW members and supporters along the way, and arrived in Florida with 30 cars – 120 people in our West Coast caravan alone.

FBI units followed us out of L.A. Agents pointed cameras at us through car windows as we left Cal State and drove east on Roscoe Boulevard to the 405 freeway. The agents were less obvious once we got on the freeway, but the FBI tracked us all the way to Miami.

The first night we stopped and laid our sleeping bags in the sand under a big sky alongside I-10 in Arizona. Nothing but endless desert in every direction. The next night, in Texas, trees dotted both sides of the road and the sky was much darker. We had no idea where we were.

We awoke to find a lovely little river not far down a gentle hill from where we slept. Everyone started whooping, hollering, tearing off our clothes, and running down the hill to jump in the water. Some grabbed bars of soap to bathe after two days on the road. There was a rope hanging from a tree branch and some of us swung out over the river and dropped in. Soon there were dozens of naked bodies and soap bubbles on the surface of that slow river. It seemed like a wonderful way to start the day, and we took it as a good sign.

It was a hot August day when The Last Patrol stopped for lunch at a Sonic burger stand in Austin. Dozens of us tried to find shade while we ate on the blacktop parking lot. One of the men – a Vietnam vet – had a knife in a sheath visible on his belt. That, we would soon find out, was illegal in Austin. I noticed and approached while a police officer was handcuffing him and asked if they could give him a citation instead of arresting him. I explained that he was part of a large group traveling through. The officer said because he was from out of state they had to take him into custody, that he would appear before a judge at 1:30 p.m., and gave me the address of the court. Luckily nobody tried to stop the officer from taking the vet to their car. As they drove away, we huddled.

It was hard to know what was really going on, why the government moved on us then and there. The Austin cop was nice enough, but we wondered if somebody was testing us, or trying to provoke us so they could beat somebody or make mass arrests. The FBI had been following us and local agencies had to know we were coming. This was Texas, with its frontier justice, after all, and our cars were painted with antiwar and anti-Nixon slogans. There were dozens of ragtag, road-weary vets and hippies converging on a fast food parking lot. We were hard to miss.

I hadn't planned to act as a lawyer on this trip. I had only activist clothes, no coat, tie, or stiff leather shoes. On this sweltering Texas day I was wearing sensible shorts and a light t-shirt, and sandals. But I had no choice. We needed this vet out of detention ASAP. We couldn't leave him in jail and we weren't leaving without him. We all had an important appointment with President Richard M. Nixon.

I was waiting in the hall with Jeannie and some vets when the courtroom opened up after its lunch break. I explained the circumstances to the clerk and asked permission to address the judge in my travel attire. I was surprised when she readily agreed. I thought maybe she'd been told to expect us, but I didn't know if that was a good or bad sign. I waited uncomfortably for the judge to take the bench. Several from our group came inside to watch. Others

70

waited in the hall. We must have made quite a scene in that small municipal court.

I was surprised again when the judge called our case right away. I became hopeful. Many judges would have made us wait and twiddle our thumbs while other cases were called. I apologized for my attire and explained that I was an attorney who was not expecting to do any lawyering on this trip, but a member of my group was arrested for openly wearing a knife in a sheath, not knowing it was against local law:

"If your honor can see fit to release this Vietnam veteran on his own recognizance, a large group of anti-war veterans can leave your town and be on our way. Otherwise we'll be stuck here for a while."

Given that choice, the judge was very kind and dismissed the charges. We left town double-time.

We drove into Houston around 6 p.m. that same evening. The freeway was under construction, so we went through a big stretch of town on surface streets. One street adjoined black working-class neighborhoods. Those sidewalks were crowded with men and women getting off busses and walking home, many with hard hats, lunch boxes, gloves, and work belts. When they saw our long line of cars with lights on and antiwar slogans, many turned and clapped. Some put their things down to use both hands.

Rush hour traffic slowed our pace, so it felt like being in a parade. In reflection, I like to think we were being honored for both aspects of our group: the "Vietnam veterans" and the "antiwar" part of VVAW. Surprised, amazed, and humbled by this reception, we felt uplifted.

The Louisiana State Police stopped us the minute we crossed the state line from Texas. A dozen State Police and unmarked cars pulled us over in the dark to the side of the road. Calling our leaders together, the officials made clear they were going to make sure nothing happened while we were in their state. To accomplish that, they were going to escort us across the entire state. We were offered no choice.

We stopped to sleep at a state park shortly after that. We picked a spot, parked our cars, and unrolled our sleeping bags. The police formed a large perimeter around us, with five officers posted as pickets all night long. VVAW, of course, always had its own sentries standing guard. We took turns. I usually took the early shift, and on this morning I saw the cops in cars, on foot, and sitting on picnic tables smoking cigarettes. They watched as we got up and got ready to leave. They escorted us all the way to the Mississippi state line.

Near Mobile, Alabama the next afternoon, as workers were getting off for the day, carloads of hard-hats filled the highway with us. White workers, we had come to expect, were often hostile to our scruffy appearance and anti-war message. One vehicle that afternoon fired a .22 into one of our cars, puncturing a door, but otherwise doing no real damage. We pulled over, had a short conference, and agreed there was nothing to do but move on and get the hell out of Alabama. Making a police report would slow us down, and might backfire on us. What good would that do?

The car I rode in encountered four black workers in the next lane. In the humid heat of that afternoon, our car windows were rolled down. The workers were drinking beer and wine on their way home. One of them, half-joking, held a bottle out the window, offering it to us. Our cars got closer together. I leaned out and grabbed the bottle. We passed it around quickly, then handed it back to our hosts, who passed us another bottle for another round. After that, we waved goodbye to each other, and held up fists of solidarity. What a great feeling!

A film crew in our caravan had driven ahead to film our cars going by. Those ground level shots wound up in two documentaries made about VVAW and the convention: *Four More Years*, by Top Value Television, and *Operation Last Patrol*, by filmmaker/actor Frank Cavestani and photo-journalist Catherine Leroy. Each film focused on Ron Kovic, whose best-selling book, *Born on the Fourth of July*, would be made into a movie starring Tom Cruise.

Kovic was driving his Oldsmobile in our caravan – 3,000 miles across the country. In Chapter 6 of his best-seller, he described looking "into the dust-covered rearview mirror and see the convoy behind me, stretching back like a gigantic snake so far I cannot even tell where it ends – cars and busses, trucks and jeeps, painted with flowers and peace signs, a strange caravan of young men wearing war ribbons on torn utility jackets and carrying plastic guns."

A big highlight of the trip took place in the Tallahassee jail, where we visited the Gainesville Eight. Arrested three months earlier, charged with weapons violations and conspiracy to riot at the Democratic National convention, they could not raise the high bail. We parked our long line of cars at the curb across the street from the jail. Over 100 of us got out of 30 cars and stood at attention on the sidewalk. Kovic and others sat at attention in their wheelchairs.

As a lawyer, I was able to visit the Gainesville Eight on behalf of our group. No need to apologize to the jail for my attire as I had in Austin. I crossed the street, entered the jail, and met with several of the defendants in an interview room. I asked how they were being treated, then told them about our caravan and our plans for Miami. I expressed the solidarity of those standing outside and the people they represented in their respective hometowns. I conveyed our support in their upcoming trial and our determination to pursue the common goal of stopping the war machine.

They asked me to spread the word that the charges were fabricated by an FBI provocateur. They were confident they would be freed. Moved by the scene outside, they thanked us and wished us success in Miami.

I emerged from the jail and walked down the steps to see our group still lined up shoulder to shoulder at attention across the street. VVAW had great discipline and deep respect for those who were sacrificing to end the war. It must have been a great sight for the Gainesville Eight, and for other inmates in that jail. It was certainly a very special moment for me.

The following year, the Gainesville Eight would be found not guilty. None of the accused put on a defense. The charges against them had been based on an undercover FBI operative who had tried to provoke violence himself. In the words of Scott Camil, one of the Eight: "We had no conspiracy to disrupt the convention. Our conspiracy, if you want to call it that, was to go down to the convention and exercise our Constitutional rights as citizens and to defend

73

those rights against anybody who tried to take away those rights, whether it be the government or anyone else. And the jury sided with us."

After my jail visit, our group camped near Tallahassee. Soon rain poured down like crazy. All of us got soaking wet within two minutes. Every low spot filled with water. Poorly placed tents and sleeping gear were soon standing in pools of water. Drenched, uncomfortable, and tired of being on the road, we stopped earlier than usual the next afternoon. The home of two solid VVAW supporters sported a huge yard. The hosts were prepared to feed more than 100 of us. They let us use their bathrooms, swimming pool and hot tub. We slept in their yard that night.

Still, I don't think our hosts were prepared for men and women tearing off our clothes, jumping in the swimming pool, and running around the yard like a bunch of kids who had eaten too much candy.

In 1972, the '60s hadn't yet ended. These Vietnam Vets, political activists, hippies, yippies, FBI informants, one lawyer – *me* – and assorted others had all been trapped in our cars, deprived of creature comforts for several days. Almost to our destination, we believed were going to stop the war. It was time to let our hair down and party.

The party didn't last long. We were too exhausted from the trip. That green lawn, that large fenced yard felt comfortable and safe compared to places we had been sleeping. The closely mown grass held fewer bugs than the uncut grasses we had camped in. I slept better that night than I had since pulling out of L.A.

On sentry duty the next morning, I awoke early, as usual. I enjoyed watching my comrades sleeping on the ground as the sky transformed from darkness to light, watching the first people slowly sit up in their sleeping bags, quietly light a cigarette, walk to the john. This night and morning in north Florida became another special memory

We stopped for lunch alongside I-95 in Jacksonville, close enough to the Atlantic Ocean to smell the sea air, completing our coast-to-coast journey. No fast-food place could seat all of us, so we ate in our cars or stood somewhere in the parking lot. We planned to join caravans from Boston and Minneapolis, then drive south to Miami as one big caravan – 100 cars and 400 people.

None of us knew where the other caravans might be. Cell phones didn't exist in those days. We posted spotters on the highway in case a caravan showed up. While discussing our dilemma, I spotted an FBI car across the parking lot. I volunteered to talk to them. One in our group thought I was crazy, but no one else objected. I cheerfully walked up to the two men seated in the car and asked if they could tell me where the other caravans were.

Normally in those days, I would have never dreamed of being friendly to FBI agents or asking them for a favor. I must have been feeling a little triumphant and correspondingly generous of spirit. The most arduous leg of our adventure was almost over. FBI agents had been with or near us at all times. (I wish now that I could see those photos they took!) By now, the FBI had to realize that we weren't going to stir the masses to revolution en route. We were only trying to make our voices heard in Miami, maybe stop the war.

We might break a few minor laws, but nothing sinister or illegal was going on. Maybe these FBI agents were feeling generous, too, because they quickly got on the radio and found out that the other caravans would be coming by on this very highway soon.

VVAW kept us disciplined and focused. I think the FBI had some grudging respect for that service, courage, organization, and dedication. It was impossible not to respect the opinion of these vets who fought in Vietnam. They had earned the right to speak and be heard.

All three caravans finally came together and stopped for the night at Daytona Beach. Hundreds of us slept on the sand. We rode into Miami the next morning, in cars and motorcycles with lights on, in single file, staying in formation as best we could. Quite a parade!

[1] Dept. of Vets Affairs, Wisconsin, *Letter of Support to VVAW*, May 12 - 15, 1972

Flamingo Park

We were greeted like heroes when The Last Patrol finally arrived at Flamingo Park. VVAW, the largest organized contingent to arrive, was respected by most everyone there. Vets greeted one another like long-lost brothers. Some of them were. As Ron Kovic described it in *Born on the Fourth of July*:

"People were dancing in the streets, playing flutes, running up to us, Yippies and Zippies shoving handfuls of joints into our laps and all the brothers were climbing out of their cars hugging and jumping on top of each other, singing and screaming and carrying on like we had just won the war."

VVAW organized an encampment with different sections and security. Others slept in areas where things were more loosey-goosey. Drugs, alcohol and anarchy were banned in the VVAW area. Yippees were prominent in other parts of the park and in the media. They questioned all rules and authority, even VVAW. Friction existed in the park, but things ran smoothly. Everyone was there for the same reasons. We were all serious in our own way.

One persistent problem, however, came in the form of off-duty Miami cops. A carload would drive by in the middle of the night and one of them would lob a tear gas canister into our sleeping areas. They didn't hide who they were or what they were doing.

I saw them quite clearly more than once. They drove in a convertible, giving them easier tosses over the bushes, tables and other barriers that encircled the encampments. Most of the off-duty police wore white tee shirts with cigarettes rolled up in the sleeve. One or two always sat up high on the back seat, like the queen's court in a parade.

Wherever the tear gas landed, we were forced to jump up and run away from the plume until it blew in another direction or dissipated. If the gas got on you, you had to find water and wash it off. A good night's sleep proved impossible.

Several information booths and tables had been set up in the park, offering literature or merchandise. But there was no legal advice available to all these people. I knew there were important things everyone should know before an event like this. Affinity groups were preparing to take action on the big day of Nixon's acceptance speech. Many prepared to break a law or two. None were getting any sound legal advice.

A flyer from the National Lawyers Guild said that a team of lawyers and law students were in town to help in case of trouble. I called the number on the flyer and asked to come in for a conversation. These young people were working out of a rented apartment. They were poorly funded, inadequately trained, and unorganized. They let me use their shower.

Their six-page *Beach Bust Book* contained too much information. Maximum sentences? Standard bail for 16 anticipated crimes? This handout was too detailed to be useful. I urged these folks to meet with affinity groups, and advise them how to avoid getting arrested, and what to expect and how to act if they did. "Leave somebody here to answer the phone," I told them, "and get out of this apartment."

After that I went around the park talking to groups about their rights, legal procedures and expectations. Some affinity groups formed around people who already knew each other. Some had been randomly assembled. Each group made its own plan and preparations, but the overall plan was to be in the streets and cause so much disruption that the Convention delegates wouldn't be able to make it back inside after dinner on the night of Nixon's acceptance speech. Our goal was for Nixon to give his speech to an empty hall, while chaos ruled outside.

The big day was just a regular workday for most people. Affinity groups hit the streets in late afternoon, as rush hour began, trying to start traffic jams that might last until 7 p.m. when Nixon was scheduled to speak. Several groups tried to make their way to the intersection that led to the front of the Convention center.

Other groups stayed on the perimeter, trying to cause traffic problems that would keep limos of delegates from getting near the convention center. One group found a small pile of telephone poles in a vacant lot and rolled some onto a major street. Other groups ran through traffic stopped at red lights, making it difficult for cars to move when the light turned green.

All these activities caused havoc here and there. The police used tear gas, batons, and, by car and by foot, chased demonstrators all over the immediate area. They were always a few steps ahead of us.

Knowing that our main goal was to obstruct the delegates returning from dinner, the police created a passageway we were unable to penetrate, thereby defeating our main strategy. They lined up scores of school busses, each bumper to bumper, touching the bus in front and in back, so nobody could squeeze between. Each bus was parked with its doors to the inside, along the passageway, forming a long wall of the windows-only sides. Inside, cops prepared to lean out those windows and swing night sticks if we got too close. In the few places where a break in the bus line opened, riot cops stood ready to protect the gap. The line of busses on either side of the street opened an avenue for the limos of delegates and dignitaries.

After hours of struggle in the streets, word spread that the hall was full. Nixon had begun his speech. We were angry, disappointed, and grumbled about what to do next. In what amounted to a makeshift public meeting, the group decided to march to the hotel where Republicans were headquartered, sit down in the street and get arrested. Right or wrong, I decided not to join that effort.

It felt to me like an act of frustration, not a clear-headed action with any real purpose. In the end, about 900 protestors filled the street in front of the hotel and got arrested. I marched alongside them, but watched from a sidewalk as they were cuffed and hauled away, one by one. It would be pointless symbolism to be number 901.

Ron Kovic and two other disabled VVAW leaders managed to get invited inside the Convention hall while the rest of us were battling the police in the streets. After shouting anti-war statements from their wheelchairs and refusing to leave, they were called "traitors," even spat on by some Republican delegates.

Most of us didn't get anywhere near the convention, of course, so we never got to meet those "patriotic" Republicans. We also never heard Kovic yelling at the top of his lungs, daring security guards to beat and forcefully drag a wheelchair-bound veteran out of the hall in front of national TV cameras. Sensibly, they decided against it.

Roger Mudd of NBC heard the shouting and commotion, and made his way through the crowd to interview Kovic. Two minutes of that interview aired on national TV that night, which we also missed.

"I gave America my all," Kovic told Mudd, "and the leaders of this government threw me and the others away to rot in their V.A. hospitals. What's happening in Vietnam is a crime against humanity, and I just want the American people to know that we have come all the way across this country, sleeping on the ground and in the rain, to let the American people see for themselves the men who fought their war and have come to oppose it. If you can't believe the veteran who fought and was wounded in the war, who can you believe?"

Born on the Fourth of July and *Operation Last Patrol* chronicle these events. The latter includes actual footage from inside the Convention.

Though none of us outside the Convention hall knew this interview was happening, it marked the high point of our trip. Everyone had a role to play. We played ours in the streets while Ron Kovic played his as our public spokesman. TV and documentary cameras captured all of it.

Retreat

The rest of us had been stymied and felt we had not achieved our main goal. We didn't know that Ron Kovic had been on the NBC *Evening News*, or that anything good had come from our efforts. We felt disappointed, and anxious to leave Flamingo Park and Miami, tired of bugs in the long grass, tear gas in the night. Most of us packed up and left early the next morning.

Maybe that attitude created bad karma. Our journey home didn't start well. We stayed together as a caravan until we reached a friendly farmhouse in Georgia, where we spent most of the day trying to regroup. I don't know about the others, but I remember feeling as if I had just escaped from Florida and now could finally relax.

We all suffered from rashes and other physical ailments from sleeping in the long grasses. We suspected the authorities purposely kept the grass unmown. On the bare ground in front of that farmhouse, experienced Vietnam veteran medics amazed me by attending to everyone in an hour. They knew how to treat platoons in the field in the shortest amount of time. The ointment they applied to my bites and rashes helped almost immediately. I started feeling better right away.

If only those medics could have solved our other problems as easily. Many of our VVAW leaders sat in jail in Miami. Some of our cars had barely made it to Miami in the first place. I rode in an old Chevy Nova from L.A., but it had broken down and was left abandoned by its owner at that farmhouse. The number of available cars had suddenly dwindled. Many of us were forced to figure out alternative ways home. We were all tired and dirty. And now the VVAW's legendary organization and discipline were breaking down.

Five of us from L.A. decided to split into groups of one or two and hitchhike to Dallas, where we would meet up hoping to find a "drive-away" car to deliver to Los Angeles. Amazingly – without cell phones or GPS – it worked out. Within a day, we all arrived in Dallas and regrouped. We shared a room for a night, took showers, made phone calls, and found an agency with a full-sized Mercury that needed to be delivered to L.A.

It was the first time I'd slept in a bed in 10 days, and only my third shower. For the next two days, we cruised across the southwest at 85mph in extravagant, air-conditioned comfort!

III

WOUNDED KNEE
AND THE
AMERICAN INDIAN
MOVEMENT

The museum at Wounded Knee.

photograph by the author

The land is sacred. These words are at the core of our being. The land is our mother, the rivers our blood. Take our land away and we die. That is, the Indian in us dies."

—*MARY BRAVE BIRD*
Lakota (1954-2013)

The Occupation and Siege of Wounded Knee — 1973

L ife was good in the Santa Barbara Legal Collective where I learned so much about law, political organizing and life. We all felt a spirit of purpose and camaraderie, and an optimism about how we could help change the world. The Selective Service cases kept me busy and brought good income into the collective, but those cases were drying up. The Paris Peace Accords, signed January 27, 1973, signaled the U.S. pullout from Vietnam. I now had the time and necessity to learn and practice other types of law.

In March, our collective attended a National Lawyers Guild weekend retreat at a remote campground in the rolling hills of the central coast, not far north of Santa Barbara. By this time there were many radical young lawyers like me, with experience combining "people's law" with political activism, and earning enough money to pay the rent and keep their offices open.

The war in Vietnam created a generation of activists who were putting energy and passion into new issues. Some new left-lawyers and legal workers at this retreat were working with the United Farm Workers in the San Joaquin Valley. Some were organizing and defending immigrants in and around Los Angeles. Others were representing militant prisoners in a rebellious prison movement: the Black Panther Party, the Weather Underground, and more.

Three young NLG lawyers from Portland came to the retreat with fresh information about the American Indian Movement (AIM), which had been in the headlines recently. Led by a group of militants from Minneapolis, AIM set out to tell the country about broken treaties and the continuing impoverishment and mistreatment of Indians at the hands of the U.S. government. In 1969, AIM participated in a take-over of Alcatraz Island (federal property) which lasted nineteen months and got a lot of attention for their cause.

In 1972 they joined with other organizations in the Trail of Broken Treaties, traveling around the country picketing, marching, rallying, and speaking at churches, meetings and local events.

The Trail of Broken Treaties grew larger and louder. It came to Washington, D.C. in November, 1972 with 500 people demonstrating and camping out on the National Mall. The Nixon administration refused to meet with the group to discuss its Twenty Point Position Paper. Feeling betrayed, the members camped out in the Bureau of Indian Affairs (BIA) offices in Washington D.C.

Some protesters went through desks and cabinets, burned files and fraudulent deeds in hallways and lobbies. After a week, they negotiated a settlement and ended the occupation with the government agreeing not to file charges and to continue treaty talks.

Several weeks later, AIM led a demonstration in Custer, South Dakota, protesting the lenient charges against a white man who killed Wesley Bad Heart Bull in a bar fight. AIM asked the trial judge to increase the charges to murder, but he refused. As the leaders left the courthouse, the police attacked the crowd. In the ensuing fight, the courthouse caught fire.

So it became big news when, on February 27, 1973, AIM and 300 followers seized the historic Wounded Knee Cemetery area of the Pine Ridge Reservation (Oglala Sioux: South Dakota). The area included the creek bed where 83 years earlier, 300 Sioux – men, women and children – were massacred by U.S. soldiers.

AIM launched the protest as a grievance against the current Pine Ridge tribal government and its leader, Richard "Dickie" Wilson, seen as a corrupt, undemocratic, and compliant tool for the Bureau of Indian Affairs (BIA). In command of the Pine Ridge tribal police, Wilson also controlled rogue goon squads to enforce his will and to punish anyone who spoke out against him.

Shots were exchanged almost immediately after AIM established a perimeter to defend a place held sacred. An armed siege against them would last 71 days. Federal marshals, FBI, BIA police encircled Wounded Knee on the first day. Personnel, weapons, armored vehicles, and military equipment moved in to prevent supplies from going in or people from getting out. Electricity was cut to discourage AIM and starve the group into submission.

But the authorities seemed reluctant to end the occupation by force. The symbolism of another attack near the site of the 1890 massacre, plus the nationwide attention that generated sympathy for the Trail of Broken Treaties made a direct attack a poor option.

The Portland lawyers told us about the siege of the AIM encampment and the arrests that were being made every day. AIM needed legal help to assist the Rapid City-based Wounded Knee Legal Defense/Offense Committee. Since the occupation might last a while, we were asked to consider sending someone to help.

At our next meeting, we determined our office was now financially stable and could afford to send one of our lawyers to South Dakota. With my draft practice fizzling out I became the logical choice. I was eager to be involved in another adventure.

I left in mid-April. The siege had entered its sixth week. One Native American, Frank Clearwater, had been shot and killed by U.S. Marshalls while sleeping in a tent the day after he arrived from the East to support the cause. My plane stopped in Salt Lake City en route to Rapid City. Several clean-cut men in crisp suits came aboard. They greeted their counterparts already on the aircraft as if they were all friends. I surmised that they were FBI and/or other federal agents heading for the same place, but to work for the other side. As the long-haired, left-wing lawyer traveling to help domestic insurgents, I sat alone, greatly outnumbered by men with guns who didn't like me.

As soon as I deplaned, I found like-minded people at Star Village, a collection of small, rectangular duplexes on a hilltop where AIM rented buildings and set up a legal office, a group kitchen, and residences.

The office labeled itself the Wounded Knee Legal Defense/Offense Committee, but from what I saw, there wasn't much offense going on. Defense took up all the energy – making lists, sorting, interviewing, representing those who were being arrested every day.

The Pine Ridge Reservation and the Wounded Knee site sit 90 miles south of Rapid City. On most nights, some insurgents tried to sneak out of the encampment, and several others tried to sneak in, bringing food, medicine and other supplies. Some from either group would get caught and arrested. Some of those who made it out would show up the next day at the office, hungry, tired, looking for a shower, a phone. After six weeks of constant siege, very little food remained inside "The Knee".

An average of 10 people were arrested each night while I was there – 1,200 during the full occupation. The federal authorities wanted to discourage any nationwide support for AIM, so they charged out-of-state folks with federal felony crimes, and required substantial bail to keep them in custody and prevent repeat attempts to help AIM. We interviewed those charged by the feds after they were transported from Pine Ridge to jail in Rapid City. We helped them contact their people, then represented them in court.

They all pleaded not guilty. We argued to get their bail lowered. The cases had been piling up and no one on either side seemed to have the time or resources to deal with these arrestees. Everyone in the system kept putting everything off day after day. This problem eventually worked in our favor: most saw their bail reduced because the jails were running out of room.

Those not charged with federal crimes were sent to the tribal jail at Pine Ridge, held on tribal crimes. All were local Native Americans because tribal courts held no jurisdiction over non-Indians. But once again, no one had the resources to deal with all these cases during the occupation. We tried to bail out as many as possible from the tribal jail, doing what we could to help them make it through another day. Each new day brought cases that went to the back of a long and growing backlog.

I quickly took on the job of bailing locals out of the Pine Ridge jail. Keeping them out of harm's way posed another problem. Viewed as AIM supporters, these locals lived on the reservation. They made easy targets for retaliation by

Dickie Wilson's goon squads. My job entailed taking $2,000 in cash to Pine Ridge every other day. I bailed out two days' worth of locals. I took them out one carload at a time, driving them to a safe spot off the reservation, often across the state line to Nebraska.

The Pine Ridge tribal government and those goon squads were tight with the BIA. Now, the FBI, U.S. Marshals and other feds ran all over town in their new jeeps, sporting new weapons, fancy radios, and "intelligence." It was not a good time or place to be a rebel.

To bail people out and do the other paperwork in Pine Ridge, I had to be admitted to practice in the tribal courts. That required my passing a test on tribal laws and rules. The entire tribal code wasn't very long. I read it in one sitting in a trailer where the "law library" had a desk, chairs, filing cabinets, and a handful of books. After I passed the test, I felt proud to have my name added to a handwritten list of lawyers admitted to practice in the Pine Ridge tribal court. It was April. Hope still survived.

Every person bailed out from the tribal jail had a case pending in the tribal court. The tribal authorities were very loose and cooperative. They were as overwhelmed as everyone else. Their jail couldn't possibly hold all those arrested. Their court couldn't deal with all the cases, so the court calendar stretched months into the future. No one knew when this might end. There always seemed to be rumors of a possible settlement.

It took most of a day to drive 90 minutes south on Highway 79 from Rapid City to Pine Ridge, pay bail and take care of paperwork in the trailer that served as the tribal police headquarters, then drive three carloads of protesters off the reservation, then drive back to Rapid City. On most days, I bailed out 10 people. Some had to spend two nights in the tribal jail because I only did this routine every other day. We didn't have the resources for me to go every day.

And I didn't want to do it every day. It was nerve-wracking to have $2000 in cash on me. It was nerve-wracking to drive carloads of insurrectionists in an area where residents were so poor and desperate that people were said to be killed for a wristwatch or less. And now this dangerous reservation was crawling with armed federal agents in jeeps, alongside tribal police and goon squads. All of them hated us.

Early in the siege, the federal authorities arrested one L.A. group as it crossed the state line from California into Nevada. Some Hollywood donors helped raise money for the group which publically proclaimed its intention to take food and medical supplies to Wounded Knee. Crossing a state line made that a federal crime. Federal agents demonstrated their intention to treat every such action seriously by jailing the arrestees, then setting a high bail for conspiracy to aid an insurrection.

Other groups acted more secretively. They made it to the area before getting caught. We called one of these groups "The Easter Bunny 13" because these students from Indiana were arrested on Easter morning crossing the state line from Nebraska. Such a large bust created a lot of work for us. We visited the jail, got names and contact information, found out whether charges would be filed, what bail had been set, and when we'd have to appear in court. When would they arrive in Rapid City so that we could begin our interviews? And what about Easter dinner?

Most of The Easter Bunny 13 trickled out of jail and came by Star Village, spending time showering and eating leftovers. One of my jobs was to pick people up at the jail and take others to and from the airport. The legal office at Star Village was the only openly acknowledged presence in town for those supporting AIM. We had to take care of every aspect of these cases.

The kitchen and office operated as a collective. Everyone shared tasks – in theory at least. Lawyers were supposed to do our share of cooking and cleaning up. We tried to make use of people who had just been released from jail, waiting for their next move, or money from home. And they were eager to help. Most left within a few days.

Lawyers and legal workers held regular meetings to discuss the work. As the occupation and siege began winding down, some of us decided to get away from the hustle and bustle of Star Village and brainstorm from a broader perspective, beyond the day-to-day processing of arrestees. NLG lawyers Norton Tooby and Jim Fennerty and I drove to Mt. Rushmore Park. We sat on the grass under the Presidents, ate lunch, and discussed the legal needs that would come after the occupation. A deal was in the works but it still looked as though AIM leaders would face serious charges. Scores of lesser cases would make it to federal court. More would be heard in tribal court. A semi-permanent legal office, with a substantial number of criminal defense lawyers and staff, would be needed.

During the 71 day siege of The Knee, more than 130,000 rounds of ammunition were estimated to have been exchanged—most by the government, of course. Two Native American occupiers died in those exchanges. Toward the end, on April 27th, Lawrence "Buddy" Lamont was shot dead by a government sniper. A local, Buddy's death fell hard on the occupiers and their supporters. They knew him, and they knew a deal was in the works. The occupation/siege was probably coming to end. Buddy's death seemed especially pointless.

Our lead lawyers, Mark Lane (author of *Rush to Judgement*) and Minnesota's Ken Tilsen, were escorted into Wounded Knee with government attorneys for negotiations with AIM leadership. The government attempted to show good faith: Buddy Lamont's funeral would be allowed to be held inside the encampment, with some outsiders permitted to bring in a traditional funeral feast for the hungry occupiers.

Buddy's body was removed from the encampment, then taken to a funeral home. A wake was held at a nearby church. People hung around the casket inside the church and the grounds outside for 24 hours. A pick-up truck arrived and unloaded a freshly killed cow onto the lawn behind the church. Women started the long process of butchering the cow and preparing huge kettles of beef stew over campfires.

The stew went into shiny new galvanized trash cans placed in the back of a pick-up truck. A slow procession walked behind the casket and the food into the encampment. The FBI searched us—even the stew—to make sure no guns or explosives were being smuggled into the compound. The trash cans held three feet of stew. Federal agents used shovel handles to poke for hidden weapons.

Inside, the occupiers tearfully hugged relatives and friends. That powerful moment filled us with both sadness and exuberance. The funeral was solemn, of course, but the feast became a joyous reunion during the long and historic struggle. Many had remained inside The Knee for the entire 10 weeks, battling danger and deprivation. A sense of relief and victory finally permeated the air.

Frances Holder and her brother Stan held posts in the leadership of the occupation. Stan took charge of the security of the perimeter. Like many Native Americans, he had served in Vietnam. Stan had been a munitions specialist. At Wounded Knee he made bomb-mines in coffee cans, burying them in strategic locations. Explosive material was in short supply. Stan directed the burial of empty coffee cans, making the FBI treat all coffee cans as bombs. AIM also had a small arsenal of guns, including AK-47s, which proved very effective at thwarting forays and deterring attacks from a distance.

Happily, the FBI never mounted an all-out attack. Soon after Buddy's funeral, a negotiated settlement was reached. The occupation ended on May 8. My office wanted me back home. I left South Dakota a few days later, but I wanted to continue helping AIM.

Leaving Santa Barbara

After returning in May, I was no longer thinking about my future in sunny Santa Barbara. For one thing I was getting island fever from being so far from L.A., the center of so much of what I was interested in. I was tired of making the long drive back and forth to spend time with my son and attend events in L.A

Politically, something was urging me to move on. For one thing, the L.A. movement matured and branched out since I left two years earlier. I knew people who were doing interesting, innovative, and important work in legal fields: immigration, prison, military, civil rights. They all worked in or passed through L.A., so that's where I wanted to be.

In Santa Barbara, I started clearing up my work. I also wanted to help AIM before getting settled back in L.A. My team in Santa Barbara knew two wealthy liberal women who gave money to worthy causes. Their definition of worthy proved to be radical in those days. These donors had given generously to the defense of the Isla Vista bank-burning defense, the Black Panther Party and the prison movement.

I wrote a simple grant proposal to fund a two-month legal stint with AIM. At the same time, I contacted AIM with news that I was trying to get back to the legal defense office temporarily toward the end of the year. I assumed they would want me in Rapid City and Pine Ridge to work on the hundreds of criminal cases that had accumulated in federal and tribal courts during the occupation.

I expected to work on tribal cases. I had been admitted to the tribal court and knew the clerks, judges, and jailers. But AIM asked me to go to Oklahoma instead. Enough lawyers had volunteered for the high-profile Wounded Knee cases in South Dakota. Rank-and-file Indians throughout the country felt ignored. Some felt angry about the attention being paid to the Pine Ridge Sioux and the "urban Indians from Minneapolis"– a derogatory reference to AIM leadership.

Oklahoma was still "Indian Country," with more tribes and Native Americans than any other state. The Indian

Removal Act of 1830 was signed by President Andrew Jackson – arguably the worst president of the 19th and 20th centuries. Between 1830 and 1850, this act forcibly removed tribes from lands they had inhabited for thousands of years. Choctaw, Cherokee, Seminole, Muscogee (Creek), and Chickasaw tribes were relocated to inhospitable land west of the Mississippi – land then thought to be worthless. In 1838 alone, the "Trail of Tears" removed more than 16,000 Cherokees from east of the Mississippi, with 4,000 dying along the route.

Several other tribes had already existed there for 200 centuries. The resettlement of new tribes forced existing inhabitants to move and make room for a huge influx of needy and unhappy survivors from the east. After the 1830 "removals," the federal government continued to force other tribes into Indian Territory – combined with the Oklahoma Territory to form the state of Oklahoma in 1907.

I remember it being an extremely hot day in late September when I left Santa Barbara. The city sparkled in the sun, every bit "the American Riviera" it labeled itself. I received the grant money I had applied for. Being used to living on very little, I had low-balled the grant request. As a result, I found myself on a tight activist-lawyer budget once again. This may have been why I didn't take my own car to Oklahama. I was afraid of driving it into the ground like that Chevy Nova we drove to Miami and abandoned in Georgia a year earlier.

I hoped to visit a friend in Alabama before reaching Oklahoma, so I searched the classifieds and found someone looking to share gas and driving duties on her trip back to Baltimore. We took I-40 East for three days before she dropped me off in Nashville. I took a bus south to Birmingham.

In those days, with my long hair, goatee and mustache, I looked like a poster boy for hippies. Waiting at the bus terminal for my friend, I began thinking nervously of the civil rights protesters who had been attacked and severely beaten in this same station during the Freedom Rides a decade earlier. Would locals lump my appearance in with all who had fought and sacrificed for Civil Rights? Would I, too, become an object of Southern hatred and violence?

Despite my original worries, I enjoyed Birmingham. One morning I spotted a '64 Plymouth Valiant convertible on the side of a highway outside the city: *For Sale – $100*. The engine ran, the brakes worked, the tires held air. This car would get me to Oklahoma, maybe even back to California.

I drove west, not knowing what to expect – from this old Valiant or the legal work that lay ahead. These two months would be unstructured. Alone, I realized I no longer had a place to call home.

Luckily, the car radio worked: lots of good rock 'n roll stations all the way to Oklahoma.

Oklahoma and the Death of Willard Brown

My first challenge was to find Stan and Frances Holder. Stan served in Vietnam and became soured on the war, racism in the military, and the U.S. government. Already upset about broken treaties and the continuing mistreatment and neglect of Native Americans, he still put on a uniform, only to confront racist attitudes toward "gooks" in Vietnam. Frances, broad minded, also saw the bigger picture beyond Oklahoma and the United States.

Stan had become a legend. His leadership in defending the Wounded Knee encampment involved the training, instruction, and the direction of the warriors. The perimeter they established worked. His military experience helped figure out how and where the federal forces would be most likely to attack. He buried explosives at choke points. Unlike the government, the occupiers had little ammunition, but Stan knew when to shoot and when to hold fire.

Out on bail and traveling after being charged, with Frances, with crimes stemming from Wounded Knee, Stan was hard to find. Authorities in South Dakota might have been anxious for all AIM militants to leave the state, but a rumored warrant from Comanche County claimed that Stan had committed assault. He may have been hiding.

One theory placed him at a sweat lodge ceremony – two to three days, plus travel. Another guess had him visiting a cousin up near Ponca City. That cousin didn't own a phone. I quickly began to understand that this project, whatever it might be, would run on an elastic basis, routinely referred to in these parts as "Indian time."

I finally tracked down Stan and Frances. Surprisingly, they had no agenda for me to follow. They knew, I think, what I couldn't: nothing we did would make a difference. Yet somehow each new generation resists injustice and struggles for their rights, and the energy is contagious!

Considering all options, we decided I should look into the recent death of a man in the Pawnee jail up near

95

Stillwater. Local police claimed that Willard Brown hanged himself in his cell, using his own belt. His tribe and family disputed that account. Witnesses at the wake and funeral had noticed injuries inconsistent with hanging, including a broken arm and extensive bruising. A history of hostile distrust between local police and Indians dictated that in addition to investigating Willard Brown's death, I would have to examine the larger issue of police mistreatment.

Stan and Frances put me in touch with the Horsechief family, leaders of the Pawnee tribe. The patriarch, Delbert Horsechief, was a respected elder and also an AIM supporter. This was unusual: the older generation of tribal leaders often opposed AIM, seeing them as hotheads and troublemakers.

Delbert's son Lance, about 20 years old, was tasked with assisting me. He had spent a year traveling all over the world with the international cast of *Up With People*, entertaining with musical performances to highlight different American cultures in the hope of bringing the world together. Wearing authentic tribal regalia, he was proud to represent his people on the world stage. He also brought his Native American history and culture to the cast, the audiences, and the people he met. His experience and training would serve us well.

Over the next two months, Lance and I visited the jail where Willard died and interviewed family members he spent time with before going to jail. We talked to those who had either known him or seen his body at the wake. The Indians remained private with outsiders. Their great respect for the Horsechief family helped open them up. Without Delbert's approval, and had Lance not been present, none of the locals would have talked candidly in my presence. And without Stan and Frances vouching for me, the Horsechiefs would never have backed my investigation.

Lance and I covered northeast Oklahoma recording interviews that I transcribed each evening. We obtained the police report and the autopsy report. We visited the Pawnee jail several times. I conducted phone interviews with a District Attorney, who read from his case file. The D.A.'s Investigator, the investigator for the state Bureau of

96

Investigation, and the FBI agent who looked into Willard's death all gave me interviews.

Their investigations were limited to reading the police and autopsy reports, plus a cursory questioning of the officers at the jail. With no digging or probing, the official story had not been questioned.

I posed one troublesome question: why had the belt not been taken from Willard, as jail regulations required? Willard had been drinking when arrested, had been in a minor fight with a family member, and expressed anger at his family. These might all be signs of a potential suicide – even more reason to take his belt away.

Other investigators noted this same discrepancy, but the officers on duty claimed not to know why the belt had not been removed.

One of the officers grew up with Willard. Although they weren't actually friends, they shared drinks together once. The police all told the same story, and seemed to bear no animosity toward Willard who, it turned out, was a regular guest in the Pawnee jail. Jailers knew him and his family well. When Willard got drunk, his family carted him to jail to sleep it off. Willard never objected to this practice. Was this routine the reason the jailers didn't remove his belt, as procedure required?

Other troublesome questions centered on the bruises and that broken arm. When and where did he get them? The police claimed they didn't know. The original autopsy noted no bruises or injuries, other than those on Willard's neck.

Within two weeks of investigation, it became clear the body would have to be exhumed. Willard had been buried for three months. And autopsies were not "the Indian way" because they desecrated the body. The original autopsy had been allowed because the family was suspicious, and they were told it was standard operating procedure. Now we would have to urge the Brown family to consent to another autopsy.

Tribal elders called a meeting. The Horsechief family argued that another autopsy would be vital to determine the cause of death. Our investigation got the tribal go-ahead.

97

The Browns gave their permission. The body could be exhumed.

To raise funds, Lance penned a letter, based on our interviews describing the customary treatment of Indians in Oklahoma:

In the last few years my Indian brothers and sisters have taken a stand to expose the living conditions of a majority of our people. Last November, the American Indian Movement made what was to be a peaceful journey to Washington, only to find and meet with violence and lies. However, documents found at that time showed that much of the chaos in our lives has been caused by the structure of the Bureau of Indian Affairs which is under the Department of Interior.

AIM also took a stand at Wounded Knee, South Dakota to show the world that there are people in this country who still haul their water, live on dirt floors, burn wood in winter, and contend with snow blowing into their homes through the gaps in the walls. Yet with all the other things in the news, it seems very hard to generate concern among the American people about the plight of the first owners of this country.

My state of Oklahoma has more Indian people than any other state. It also has more prejudice, discrimination and exploitation than any other state. Like the people in the Pine Ridge Reservation in South Dakota, we tried many legal and peaceful ways of helping our people. We get very impatient and discouraged, but we do not give up.

The Indian people of my town of Pawnee have faced many kinds of problems over the years since we were forced to come here from Nebraska. Our boys have been kicked out of school recently for wearing their hair in a way that threatens school officials. We have had valuable land stolen from us by the city of Pawnee. Local officials have used the "legal system" to try to make our Council ineffective while they hope for the election of people they can "work with" easier.

We recently went to the county jail to visit an Indian man who was arrested for public drunkenness. As the Sheriff let us in he said, "Elmer likes it here. He gets three meals a day and a warm place to sleep." But when we talked to Elmer, he wanted very much for us to try to get him out as soon as possible. The Sheriff's attitude is typical of the feelings of white people here towards our Indian people.

These attitudes show up when the police see an Indian who has been drinking. That man will be arrested. If a white man has been drinking the same amount, he would not be arrested. Most of the Indian people in Pawnee had personal experience or have close relatives and friends with personal experience of police brutality. Some women in town have also been told that they wouldn't be arrested (for public drunk) if they would go into an alley and "cooperate."

Indeed, Lance and I had studied both the county and city dockets of arrests over the past year and found that two-thirds of the total charges and over three-quarters of the public drunkeness charges were filed against Indians, who comprised only 16% of the population. Non-Indians were arrested mainly for traffic offenses.

Because of my long, blond hair, goatee, and mustache, Lance and his friends took to calling me *Mr. Custer*. We spent several evenings at dances and social events, and at a lake where we drank beer, smoked cigarettes, shot the breeze. One Saturday afternoon, while drinking beer and watching college football on TV, a man walked into the room with a long needle in one hand and a cork in the other. "Who doesn't have a pierced ear?" he asked.

The author and his son, Demian.
July, 1973

All eyes fixed on me. If that man – or me, Mister Custer – had been sober, I might have a straight hole through my ear lobe. It's not straight.

Oklahoma is a big state. We frequently had to drive long distances. My Alabama license plates expired in August. The tags carried 1973, so I hoped the car would be considered legal until the end of the year, when I could register it back home, but as a radical lawyer for AIM, I had probably been under surveillance during much of my stay. So when state troopers pulled me over in a mild snowstorm some two hours southwest of my apartment, I figured it wasn't just another traffic stop. I was right.

The troopers pulled me over for expired tags, here on a rural stretch of highway in the middle of an empty landscape. They refused to give me a fix-it ticket. Instead, they impounded my car. Making matters worse, they refused to give me a ride to the impound yard at Anadarko. Forced to hitchhike back to Stillwater, I couldn't stop thinking that my apartment was probably being searched.

Without a car, I made phone calls, sent checks, managed to get my car registered in California, and had the documents mailed to me. Lance then drove me to Anadarko to retrieve the Valiant.

A sympathetic pathologist in Oklahoma City agreed to perform another autopsy of Willard – for free. With his signature on the required form, I drove to the County medical examiner's office in Pawnee for his signature, then on to Oklahoma City for the Medical Examiner's sign off. That accomplished, the legal exhumation of Willard's body could begin.

Early one December morning, Lance and I drove to the Ponca City cemetery in a pick-up with several young men. We began to dig with only shovels, gloves, and lots of rope. It was cloudy and windy. Few leaves remained on the trees. The damp earth and the desolate scene seemed perfect for digging up a body. No one noticed or cared about us on that ghostly morning.

We finally uncovered the casket. Recent rains and the weight of wet soil had created suction on the bottom of the casket. It took hard work to loosen the grip of the grave. With ropes, we lifted it out of the deep hole, loaded it into the back of the pick-up. The tailgate shut. We drove south on I-35 to Oklahoma City, Willard Brown in his casket in the truck bed.

My lower back has never been the same since that morning.

I sometimes faint at the sight of x-rays and needles. Blood has the same effect on me. Naturally, I was chosen to observe the autopsy.

The procedure violated the tribal religion and sensibilities. The tribe didn't trust the authorities, so somebody had to watch to make sure there were no irregularities – no funny business. Even if I didn't faint, how would I know what funny business looked like?

I didn't faint. I watched closely, took notes, acted serious, hoping I wouldn't betray the depth of my cluelessness. It felt bizarre. And Willard Brown had been in the cold ground for three months. I'll spare you – and myself – the gruesome details.

You Are Under Arrest

They kept Willard's body at the hospital overnight. Next morning, we slid the casket into the pick-up and drove back to the Ponca City Cemetery. Several cop cars greeted us. They waved us to a stop at the side of an interior road, then excitedly explained that we violated the law by exhuming the body the day before. And I was under arrest. And we would not be allowed to enter the cemetery or re-bury the body without going through proper procedures.

I showed the officer-in-charge the exhumation form with all three required signatures. The police calmed down and huddled to discuss the matter.

They informed us that even though we had obtained the required permissions to exhume the body, we had not obtained the permission of local police or the cemetery management. And I would not be arrested right now. And we still could not bury Willard.

I decided to bluff. Knowing the tribe would never approve, I told the officer-in-charge, "Okay, we'll leave this casket here by the side of the road and let you put it back in the ground. Merry Christmas."

Stunned, the officer raised a hand. "Wait a minute."

After huddling again, they told us we would be allowed to enter the cemetery, re-bury Willard, even conduct a short ceremony.

From all the interviews I had conducted, and through getting to know Willard's story and meeting his family and friends, that short ceremony proved very moving to me. This was the second Indian funeral I attended that year. Both took place under memorable circumstances.

The autopsy turned up nothing conclusive, no broken arm, no unusual bruising. It was difficult to tell, and it all looked unusual to me. There was nothing more I could do. My time and grant money were running out. The back pain from the digging and lifting had me doubled over on the floor for days.

I packed up before Christmas and drove west on I-40 just as one of the first winter snow storms hit the Texas panhandle, the mountains of New Mexico and northern Arizona.

I arrived back in SoCal in time for Christmas, with cowboy boots from Oklahoma for my three-year-old son, and stories to tell. My lower back still ached. I fell sick in bed with a winter bug. I needed to find a place to live. I needed to start a new chapter of my life. But not today.

I ended my memorable year holed up in a Burbank motel watching TV. I was back in L.A. And one of these days, I would start feeling better.

IV

IMMIGRATION
AND
CIVIL RIGHTS
LOS ANGELES AND BEYOND

International Border fence, San Diego
photograph by the author

*Recognize yourself in he and she who are
not like you and me.*

— CARLOS FUENTES

Fighting *La Migra*

The L.A. political scene had changed while I lived in Santa Barbara. A generation of activist law students now struggled to understand the Vietnam War and colonialism, and offered a radical critique of our country and how much it needed to change. They were graduating, trying to figure out what to do with their lives and their new skills. Legal collectives offered an attractive setting to cut their teeth as lawyers, become more effective as political people living their politics – maybe make a difference.

Early in the new year, I began searching for a place to live and a way to support myself. I found a small apartment in Los Feliz near Marshall High School, a duplex of sorts – a small one-story stucco building in front of the owner's home on busy Hyperion Avenue. A woman and her young daughter lived in the other half of this small building. We both considered it temporary.

My first visits were to Steve Hollopeter at CASA (*Centro de Acción Social Autónomo* – Center for Autonomous Social Action) and Steve Orel at the local National Lawyers Guild office.

I had met Steve Hollopeter in 1963 during Frosh Camp, the orientation week for new freshmen at UC Santa Barbara. We didn't really get to know each other until the Lawyers Guild convention in 1971 in Boulder, when Steve, Barbara Honig, Gary Silbiger and I drove back to L.A. together.

Steve's dad, a successful Pasadena criminal defense lawyer, represented rich and high-profile clients. Steve renounced a life of luxury. A star football player in high school, he chose to live, work, drink, and smoke pot with the struggling immigrants. He loved Mao's dictum to "serve the people," but he didn't want to serve from a fancy office.

He lived in a room within a large old Victorian house near the University of Southern California (USC). The commune served as a flop-house, safe house, and a way station for newly-arrived immigrants and others just passing through. Steve had devoted the past few years helping the Mexican and Central American immigrants who, he explained, came to L.A. to escape the poverty and hopelessness imposed by an international economic system dominated by the U.S. A few years, later refugees would flee from U.S.-fueled civil wars in Central America.

A recent graduate of Southwestern Law School, Steve was organizing NLG students to defend immigrants in deportation hearings. He discovered a little-known fact in the INS (Immigration and Naturalization Service) regulations: non-lawyers could represent people in deportation hearings. Southwestern opened a teaching legal clinic–the Community Legal Assistance Center–to train law students eager to help, anxious to get the experience law school didn't offer. Steve and his disciples drove INS judges crazy.

In 1974 Steve was working out of CASA, started by two legendary organizers: Humberto "Bert" Corona and Chole Alletore. Bert and Chole each had a long history of organizing workers. Bert was a founder of the Mexican American Political Association (MAPA) in 1960, Hermandad Mexicana Nacional and the Brown Berets.

Housed in a two-story on Pico Blvd. west of Vermont, CASA maintained offices, meeting rooms, and a large kitchen. The biggest need for those newly arrived in a strange country centered on filling out immigration papers. Bert and Chole empowered immigrants to support and run their own organization. Individuals and families paid membership dues, received help with jobs, landlord issues, medical aid, wage recovery, and received legal advice.

Steve learned Spanish to help with whatever legal problems he could, mostly deportations and appeals. He believed Mao's respect for the masses meant that everyone was considered equally worthy of freedom, security, and the necessities of life. That included respecting the experience and opinions of peasants. However uneducated a person might be, she or he had an important story and point of view. Steve's enthusiasm helped propel Barbara, Gary and me to study Marxism more thoroughly.

I hadn't seen much of Barbara or Gary since that trip home from Boulder. They had been students in L.A. then, while I was a new lawyer in Santa Barbara. Law students Carlos Villanowith, Alan Wernick, Mario Vasquez and John

Grant also worked in the CASA legal office. John had been Student Body President at UCSB when I worked in the Santa Barbara legal collective. Alan & Mario shared an apartment not far from CASA. We went to their place almost every day after work to smoke pot, drink beer, and talk for hours about the myriad threads of our human and political fabric.

Gary and I formed a CASA legal collective called Eiden, Rodriguez & Silbiger (alphabetical order again). We handled deportation hearings, appeals, and legal matters the trained volunteers couldn't take on.

Antonio Rodriguez hailed from a large family of East L.A. political and social activists, all well connected and respected in East L.A. and Boyle Heights. He spent his childhood hustling in the streets of Juarez while his father toiled in the fields of Texas and California, sending money back across the border. The family finally came to the U.S. when Antonio was 14. In 1968, he became one of the first Chicanos admitted to UCLA law school under a new Equal Opportunities Program.

As a law student, Antonio played a big role in the defense of Los Tres del Barrio, three local guys busted for drugs while working as drug counselors. The community felt the police were really out to discredit the counseling program, and that the three were set up or singled out because they stood up for the rights of the young people. Antonio led a committee that worked to defend the three before and during the trial, and he worked on the appeal until their sentences were reversed and reduced.

Though not as involved in day-to-day work of the CASA cases as the rest of us, Antonio's involvement and his name on the letterhead meant a lot. He played a role in the governance and internal politics within CASA and the Latino community beyond.

Around this time, I was becoming more involved in the NLG. It was growing, increasingly involved in several important issues. I volunteered to help in the NLG office, run almost single-handedly by Steve Orel, a friendly school drop-out. A hippie with long hair and a perpetual "mellow" smile, Steve came across as one of those "natural high" guys who had "dropped out of school and into life" – no drugs, preferring tea, classical music and good vibes.

The two Steves – Orel and Hollopeter – worked with enthusiastic NLG students, most from Loyola and Southwestern law schools. Many in the NLG at this time read and talked about Marxism, intent on using their legal training & skills to serve the people, not just the rich. Several radical collectives emerged around the country, including the Bar Sinister, a legal collective in L.A. closely affiliated with the NLG, and the Santa Barbara Legal Collective that I helped found.

Student volunteers wanted to know more about working collectively in a cooperative structure of equals, struggling for change in themselves and society. I was happy to share what I knew. The custom of the new left required that we would go around the room and tell our personal stories. We called it "class history." We always included our evolution as political activists. Lifelong friendships were forged in those long meetings.

Early in 1974, the Bar Sinister started a Marxist study group with a dozen people. The group doubled, then doubled again. Eventually over 40 people moved through three courses of study. Young activists were hungry for answers on what was wrong and what they could do about it. For one brief moment, the radical left in L.A. stood unified. It felt wonderful.

CASA Reunion, 2018
l to r: The author, Antonio Rodriguez,
Gary Silbiger

CASA
and Deportation Hearings

Some of us spent our work days in a second-floor office at CASA–*Oficina Legal*. To call it modest would be an understatement: old linoleum floors, bare light bulbs, mismatched furniture, political posters in Spanish – Zapata, Che–thumb-tacked to the walls. Downstairs, a commercial kitchen held two large refrigerators and three stoves. Every morning and afternoon a team of volunteers cooked for those working in the building and for others in need. Dinner was served around 4 p.m. on two long tables in the dining area.

I benefited by learning a little about Latino cultures and cooking in those days. The mostly female volunteers came from Mexico, Guatemala, Nicaragua, Honduras, and El Salvador. They spoke the language of chicken soup. Whole pieces of chicken got mixed with big pieces of every vegetable available, spiced with lemon and cilantro, served with rice, beans, and corn tortillas. Done with immigration court by mid-afternoon, I could relax with a good meal and good people.

The volunteers also made breakfast every morning. That meal started with eggs, rice, beans, and corn tortillas heated on a large griddle. That time of day kept me busy with reviews of the daily files, the start of a dreaded struggle ahead. Most of our clients didn't have a chance. Most days, I left that breakfast table with my stomach in knots.

Each morning I drove downtown to immigration court. Most of our cases, sadly, felt hopeless. Immigration judges hated me, Steve Hollopeter, and our clients. The judges came across as pompous, callous, unschooled, and disdainful of immigrants and lawyers who took their cases. Apparently, it was one thing to represent a client for money, but another thing to believe in and fight for them as human beings with families.

The Immigration and Naturalization Service fueled an assembly line for throwing "illegal aliens" out of the country. Immigration Court judges didn't like anyone or anything that challenged or slowed that momentum. We wondered if they had more important appointments to keep –dentist, a haircut, golf. Most immigration lawyers became regulars, going along with the program, getting it over with, going to lunch, then back to the office.

Immigration prosecutors were called trial attorneys. They opposed everything I tried to do, and wanted to obtain a deportation order quickly. I didn't want to do anything quickly. This proved to be an irreconcilable conflict. Trial attorneys wanted our clients out of the country ASAP. I wanted to delay their hearings and keep them here and working, supporting their families. Judges and trial attorneys saw each other every day. They worked closely together, and often appeared to be old friends – perhaps because most of the immigration judges had once been trial attorneys. We questioned the fairness of that system. All the rules stacked up against the immigrants and those who defended them.

Only a small percentage of immigrants arrested actually received deportation hearings because most agreed to "voluntary departure." Many of our clients held jobs, made car payments, had kids in school, mouths to feed. They had been here a while, had friends and connections, wanted and needed to avoid deportation. Through our training, CASA members knew about their legal rights. Most them knew what to do when arrested. Those I represented were instructed to refuse to sign voluntary departure forms. They posted bail or were released on their own recognizance, and went back to work.

Clients usually came to us with a hearing date set by the Border Patrol, not the Immigration Court. I would send a letter to the court noting that I would be their lawyer and would be unavailable on that given day – whenever it might be. My request for a continuance noted several days when I would be available, typically two or three months off. This didn't pose a major problem. Deportation hearings jammed the docket. The next opening would no doubt be months anyway. Delay stood at the center of my strategy. I took as much advantage of it as I could.

In a typical deportation hearing, a trial attorney would ask the client two questions: "Where were you born?" "What is your country of citizenship?"

Clients would be instructed to answer honestly. The trial attorney's case would be made. In a deportation case, being born outside the U.S. equated to proof beyond a reasonable doubt. In most cases, nothing else mattered.

But I wondered why clients wouldn't be better off invoking their Fifth Amendment right against self-incrimination. Wouldn't the trial attorney then be required to find some other way to prove place of birth and citizenship? The standard answer I received cited the civil nature of deportation hearings. Fifth Amendment rights apply in criminal cases. Immigration judges believed that defendants had to answer the two main questions. That led to a quick, slam-dunk hearing and certain deportation.

After consulting with Steve, Gary, Antonio and others, I started advising clients to invoke the Fifth Amendment. I told them what that meant, and exactly how to say, "I refuse to answer because it might incriminate me." Judges and trial attorneys hadn't encountered this tactic in routine cases. They reacted with disbelief and outrage. The judges yelled and threatened both me and my clients: "You can't invoke the Fifth Amendment in a civil proceeding!"

Our clients were already upset and afraid of a man in authority (the Immigration Court judges were all male). Angry and yelling judges made matters worse. Many clients wanted to give in to this intimidation. It was hard to keep them from giving up. I quickly learned that it helped to have them say, "On advice of my attorney, I refuse to answer. . ." That shifted the blame to me. It was the truth.

Knowing nothing about immigration law when I began at CASA, I read the laws and regulations carefully and stumbled on some details that most had not seemed to notice. Some obscure sections came in handy right away. Some would also prove helpful years later in Tulsa.

My review of the laws and regulations revealed several questionable criminal provisions in Immigration Law. All were rarely used. Any "illegal alien" not in possession of an alien registration card was guilty of a misdemeanor. Most undocumented immigrants had never owned alien registration cards in the first place. What sense did this provision of the law make? Moreover, the feds didn't want to hold anyone in criminal jails only to take them to federal criminal court for minor and technical crimes, when these same folks could simply be deported in a heartbeat? That, I was learning, is precisely what had been happening decade after decade. My research showed that this provision of the law had only been used eight times!

Still, the 1934 law remained on the books. It gave us a hook to hang our Fifth Amendment hat on. After several painful hearings, we won some appeals. Immigration Courts were forced to honor a defendant's right to remain silent because of the potential for criminal prosecution under this little-known law.

The trial attorney could easily eliminate the Fifth Amendment objection by getting a letter from the U.S. Attorney granting the person immunity from criminal prosecution for their testimony. Why not, these technical crimes weren't being charged anyway? They could even get a stack of such pre-signed letters to be filled in by the trial attorney in each case. But that seemed to be out of the question for a dysfunctional bureaucracy – too much trouble, I guess.

The Immigration Court judges and trial attorneys didn't like our Fifth Amendment pleadings. They didn't like me for upsetting their cozy way of doing things. During one heated argument, a judge yelled at me: "Keep the Constitution out of my courtroom!" If he believed the Constitution did not apply to undocumented immigrants, he was wrong. The Bill of Rights protects "persons," not just "citizens." The Supreme Court has upheld that repeatedly since our country was founded.

I also discovered that Immigration Court judges had no contempt power. They could not summarily punish me for perceived disobedience or disrespect. They could only recommend that I be barred from practicing in Immigration Court. That would involve a lengthy process. It would also require actual, not just perceived, misconduct on my part. And that would have to be reviewed by higher courts.

It offended me how Immigration Court judges treated our clients and anyone who bucked the system. I decided that when these judges gave me crap or raised their voices or said something rude or disrespectful, I would respond in equal measure. They were shocked when I started talking back and wouldn't stop when told to do so, but they quickly found out they could do nothing about it.

I limited my responses to the judges. If they tried to take action against me, I could prove by way of the recorded hearing that I had been provoked. I had not done or said anything worse than the judge had. Rude and arrogant behavior had become a habit with most of the Immigration Court judges, so I found myself talking back mostly to the worst ones.

A high point came when an Immigration Court judge kept insulting me as he walked from his courtroom into a large secretarial area next door. I followed him in and responded to each comment and insult he made. At first, the secretaries tried to ignore us. Soon everyone who worked in the Immigration Court stopped what they were doing to listen to his Great Arrogance answered by my Great Impudence.

I liked getting in their faces, exposing their pomposity, showing my contempt. It felt as if it was about time somebody did! On the other hand I was worn down by being hated and treated rudely day after day. This was only the surface of an inherently unfair, out of date, unnecessarily complex, callous system that disrespected the poorest and most vulnerable among us. In the same way our capitalist economy views people as consumers and dollars, INS sees immigrants as numbers. I psyched myself up every morning on my way to the eighth floor of the Federal Building.

Walking down that long hall from the elevators to the Immigration Court, I reminded myself, "You can do it.

Whatever happens, it will be over by noon. Who cares what these assholes think or say?"

But every morning was difficult, ugly, stomach-wrenching.

When the court finally accepted that it couldn't make my clients testify, trial attorneys started introducing Form I-213 into evidence. This form was routinely filled out by the border patrol agent at the time of arrest, similar to a police report. Agents asked about country of birth and citizenship, then recorded the answers on the I-213. Most of the immigrants answered truthfully. Once accepted into evidence, Form I-213 would be sufficient to establish deportability.

I objected to the form on hearsay grounds. The document did not speak for itself. Testimony from the arresting agent would be necessary to authenticate the document and establish that it reflected a true and accurate record of what had been said. The Border Patrol agent would also become subject to cross-examination. Of course, INS stood opposed to bringing an agent to court for every one of my deportation hearings. If they did it for me, they would have to do it in every case, for every defense lawyer.

At first, judges simply overruled my objection and accepted the I-213 into evidence, then issued a deportation order. We appealed each time, buying time for our client. Once again, we started winning reversals in the Board of Immigration Appeals. Just as before, those deportation orders were reversed. The cases were returned to Immigration Court "for further proceedings."

Trial attorneys, judges and Border Patrol agents hated this ruling. Many cases got delayed due to uncertainty and resistance. All of this surprised the Border Patrol. Agents often couldn't attend a hearing on the court's schedule. They weren't used to scheduling court hearings on their calendars. Going to court, testifying in routine deportation cases upset their routine. They worked in the field. They had factories and apartments to raid, businesses to crack down on, jails to visit, leads to follow.

I didn't mind bringing Border Patrol agents into court. I didn't approve of U.S. immigration policies, so I would have gladly pulled all of INS out of the field. When an agent didn't show up, I would get a long continuance. When that hearing finally took place, I objected to as much as I could, raising as many issues as possible for an appeal. After making an official record – mainly through objections – I would turn the case over to our appellate department: Steve, Gary, and our law students.

Appeals dragged on. INS was inefficient at all levels. One of my cases got misplaced for five years. The whole time, my client was out on bail, working and living his life.

The more issues I could raise in a hearing, the more chance we had to extend the appeal, maybe win a new hearing. We won quite a few appeals because judges had denied motions I made and rights I asserted without giving them genuine consideration. Most judges found my motions absurd and dismissed them out of hand.

They were wrong. A lot. Some of our cases were included in the Board of Immigration Appeals reports. Other lawyers soon started advising their clients to invoke the Fifth Amendment, and to object to admitting any Form I-213. I went around believing that INS hated me.

Years later – sometime around 1990, as I recall – I was asked to appear for L.A.'s Central American refugee center. One of its clients was being held at a detention facility at the border. I was living near San Diego then, so it sounded easy. I just needed to request bail for a man with a good work history and a stable family life in the U.S.

When the case was called, the Immigration Court judge asked me to approach the bench. He said he had been an immigration trial attorney in L.A. when I was practicing there. He wanted me to know that he admired how we fought for our clients in those days.

Stunned, I teared up and stammered a soft thank-you, then stepped back. The judge ordered the client released on his own recognizance.

Outside, all those memories came flooding back – the decisions and difficulties in Immigration Court. It took me a while to realize what I was feeling: validation.

Iran and the Fall of The Shah

We cannot live only for ourselves. A thousand fibers
connect us with our fellow men; and among those fibers,
as sympathetic threads, our actions run as causes, and
they come back to us as effects. — HERMAN MELVILLE

I served as a legal observer at a demonstration of the Iranian Students Association (ISA) in Beverly Hills in March, 1975. The Left had common cause with ISA. Both wanted to expose the Shah of Iran as an example of a corrupt dictator supported by the U.S. for geopolitical reasons. Support for dictators like the Shah revealed the hypocrisy of the U.S. narrative that our government promotes peace and democracy. ISA wanted the monarchy overthrown and democracy restored to an ancient and proud people.

ISA marched. A scuffle occurred with security at the Beverly Wilshire Hotel. Windows were broken in public areas. Glass littered the floor, but the damage appeared minimal. Still it created quite a scene and disruption for guests in a venerable luxury hotel. Several ISA activists and supporters were arrested and charged with crimes, both misdemeanors and felonies.

The Shah, Mohammad Reza Pahlavi, was the son of a general who declared himself Shah (king) in 1925. Reza Shah was forced to abdicate by the allied forces in 1941. He had supported the Nazis. His son, the Shah-in-waiting, knew better than to antagonize the allies. When Iran's democratically elected Prime Minister, Mohammad Mosaddegh, nationalized Iran's oil industry in 1953, both the U.S. and U.K. backed a coup. Mosaddegh was killed. The Shah was placed back on the Peacock Throne – taken as a trophy of war with Delhi in 1739 by Persia's Nadir Shah. The U.S. and U.K. needed Iran in the Cold War now. Because of its size, strategic position, and influence, Iran was pivotal to the region. The Shah received U.S. financial and military support, despite his reputation for corruption and repression.

I became the lead lawyer for the felony defendants. In the process, I got to know several Iranian activists, especially two of the leaders. We held defense meetings, went to court together, and generally saw a lot of each other. The ISA leaders were anxious to educate the world about Iran. They impressed me with their intelligence and dedication. As they explained the history and politics of Iran, I became even more impressed. We resolved all criminal cases with a favorable plea bargain. In exchange for pleading no contest to a misdemeanor, with no fine or jail time, the remaining charges were dismissed.

I was home in Huntington Park one Saturday when one of the ISA leaders, Zia, called to ask if he could come over for a visit. This struck me as curious. Our case had ended. And he was a political friend, someone I would see at meetings, political events and demonstrations, not socially, and not at my home. In his 40's and older than most of us, Zia offered wisdom and patience to younger and less committed activists. He also owned an unquenchable anger and an impatience about the continuing injustices he saw in the world. He and the ISA leadership were anti-Soviet communists. They were also internationalists who saw Iran as a microcosm of a big world with a long history of injustices.

After pleasantries, Zia and his friend, Reza, asked me to fly to Iran on their behalf for an indefinite period. I should leave as soon as possible. Eleven dissidents had been arrested by the Shah's secret police, SAVAK, and were going on trial for treason, punishable by death.

ISA wanted me to attend that trial. If denied access, I was to make a fuss about Iran's lack of openness and due process. If nothing else, my presence as an outside observer might create a salutary effect, whether or not I would be admitted to the proceedings.

ISA hoped to shine some light on this case and limit the Shah's government from doing whatever it wanted to the defendants. The Shah had to know that the world was watching. Exiles and students in other parts of the world also committed to sending observers to focus attention on the brutality of the dictatorship. We all hoped to make a difference.

My Iranian friends couldn't accompany me to Iran. The Shah might jail, torture, even kill them with impunity.

Zia and Reza were known enemies of the regime, so we had to assume I would be watched. Any Iranian who accompanied or worked with me would be suspect. They warned caution. I, too, could get jailed or killed just for pissing someone off.

My U.S. citizenship should have provided a measure of protection, but I couldn't take anything for granted. I would be alone in a strange country, run by a government that would like me silenced. My own government might not care, but our embassy might be obliged to help me should I wind up in trouble. Or if I managed to disappear.

This was one of those opportunities.

Iran 1976

The trial might start any day. I landed in Tehran, a sprawling city on the south side of a snow-capped mountain range dominating the landscape. Our flight was scheduled to stop in Beirut, but in January, 1976, a civil war began in Lebanon. The Beirut airport closed to regular flights the day before I was slated to land there. Even before getting to Iran, I had to find an alternate route.

The Shah still held the country in an iron grip. His SAVAK forces were everywhere. Largely dependent on the U.S. since 1953, the Shah benefited from having Iran's military and secret police trained and supplied by the U.S. My government stood as the Shah's main source of power.

And now, the Shah was modernizing and westernizing his country. Iran was open for business, heavily militarized, and a major supporter of U.S. political and military interests in the Middle East. On the positive side, women had been given more freedoms, and the economy was good because of U.S. military aid, and changes to agriculture which replaced crops to feed the people with pistachios for export to Europe. In Tehran, for example, women attended school, wore western dress openly, drove cars, and even went to bars.

I checked into the modest Hotel Elizabeth near the center of the capital. Without knowing this city, its government or the language, I realized the difficult assignment I had volunteered for. My ISA friends didn't provided any contacts. They feared that would jeopardize those I contacted. I was on my own.

Luckily, downtown was laid out in rectangles and grids. The taxi system made it easy to get around. Most taxis cruised the major streets, picking up and dropping off passengers along the way, like busses without regular stops. Checking my map, I would take a taxi until it intersected the street I needed to get to, then I'd take another taxi to my destination. Any taxi with room for at least one person would pick me up. Most places could be reached in two or three rides.

I started with the most obvious government agency – the justice department. After attempts to put me off, an official finally met with me. Cordial and polite, he invited me to share coffee, explaining that the government had nothing to do with the upcoming military trials. He claimed to be extremely sorry he couldn't help me. I pressed for names and phone numbers of those who might help. I got the Iranian run-around. This routine repeated itself at other governmental offices. I asked the U.S. Embassy for help. They told me they'd get back to me.

I was, of course, calling attention to myself with all the phone calls and appointments. That was part of my intention. I felt certain I was being watched and that my hotel phone had been tapped. I convinced myself that one or more of the smiling folks who worked at Hotel Elizabeth would be reporting to SAVAK on my comings and goings. I also sensed I was being followed when I walked the streets. I worried I might be found in a ditch, so I wrote daily reports of where I went, who I talked to. I made copies with carbon paper, keeping the original and mailing the copy back home each day. I walked to post offices in roundabout ways so as not to be followed. I probably failed.

When I ran out of phone numbers to call and appointments to make, I went to the easiest place to strike up conversations with strangers – bars. Iranians seemed friendly yet guarded when it came to political and social issues. None of them knew me. I was drinking Star beer, but I could have been a governmental plant. Or CIA.

Some people hinted they didn't like the Shah but would not come right out and say that. I spotted several winks and knowing looks. One man wrinkled his face and shook his head at the mention of the Shah's name. With nothing I could quote, I still got general confirmation of the atmosphere of fear and repression my ISA friends had told me about.

Iranians loved talking about the U.S. Many had visited or had plans to visit, even move there to be with relatives or join business ventures. I felt like an outsider among the many westerners in town. I guessed that they were part of the evil system my friends were hoping to overthrow.

One day the front page of my morning newspaper announced that the trial had begun the day before. I had left my phone number with everyone I called or saw in person, but no one called to inform me about the trial, much less invite me to attend. Like everyone else, I learned the news after the fact.

The lead article stated the government's case and its intention to seek the death penalty. Nothing indicated the location of the trial. In a frenzy, I started calling everyone I could think of to get that most basic information. No luck. Only rumors: some military facility out of town was hosting the trial. I received apology after polite apology from those who claimed not be in a position to help me.

The next day, the headline pronounced that the trial had concluded. All 11 defendants had been found guilty. Ten had been sentenced to death!

The next morning, the newspaper reported that the 10 executions had been carried out!

The ISA was active in many countries, raising awareness about the true nature of the Shah's regime, laying the groundwork for change. I flew to Rome where I was met by Iranian students who arranged for me to speak to a group of leftist legislators. I spent a night in Rome, then onto to Frankfurt, where I was met by more Iranian students who put me on a train to Aachen.

The train ride along the Rheine traveled the sloping hills of a green river valley with castles here and there. Pulling into the station in Aachen, the smell of chocolate from nearby factories overwhelmed me. I quickly got used to it.

I spent a few relaxing days in Aachen, leisurely walking around town by myself each day. Humans found the area about 5,000 years ago, drawn by warm mineral springs. Charlemagne called this beautiful city home. His remains are interred in the cathedral he built in 786 A.D. German kings after Charlemagne continued to be crowned in Aachen.

In addition to walking, I read for pleasure, unwound, and thought about my experience in Tehran. My hosts didn't speak much English. They spent most of their time speaking Farsi. They wanted to hear the details of what I'd seen and heard, of course, and after two weeks completely alone in Iran, I was only too happy to have someone to talk to.

By now I felt very much at home with young, leftist Iranians, whether they spoke English, Italian, or German as their second language. They seemed the same whether they lived in SoCal, Germany or Italy. They played backgammon for hours. Intelligent, sophisticated, witty, and fiercely dedicated to freeing their country from western domination, they committed themselves to wresting Iran from the dictator who called himself King of Kings.

No matter what country we were in, we spoke the same language of the international proletariat – Marx, Engels, Lenin, and Mao. It was great for me to be around political people like them. At home, I spent much of my time talking to people about our inconsequential cultural and consumer things. We did not immerse ourselves in world issues 24/7 like these exiles.

I flew to Stockholm. My mother's parents had each been born and raised in Sweden, and spoke Swedish to each other. Proud of her heritage, my mother kept Scandinavian knick-knacks around the house (*Uff Da*) and belonged to Scandinavian clubs. I looked forward to my only visit to my grandparents' homeland.

But this was a one night stand, as Rome had been. I picked up very little local flavor. Just a month earlier, I had never been outside North America and had no plans to go anywhere. Now I'd visited Tehran, Rome, Germany, and Stockholm.

I stayed close to the Iranian students after my trip. I made personal speaking appearances about my experiences and observations, and commented on the bigger picture of Iran and the world. I met and played backgammon with ISA students in Ames, Iowa, Lawrence, Kansas, Houston and Oklahoma City. ISA continued to hold protests and educational events to keep the repressive puppet regime in the public consciousness. As my trip became old news, I got back to my life and other political issues

CLAC and Kathy

Southwestern Law School hired me in 1976 to supervise students in an in-house legal clinic serving the poor near MacArthur Park. Community Legal Assistance Center (CLAC) was started by NLG law students, including my friends Steve Hollopeter, Barbara Honig and Gary Silbiger. They volunteered their new knowledge and skills by serving the people. They asked for help from Southwestern, which gradually converted the clinic into a teaching tool.

When I arrived, four supervising attorneys and four offices made up the Clinic. Each office had a paid student director – someone in her/his second year of working here – and an assistant director in the first year of service. Each office had a staff of a dozen students to handle minor legal-aid cases, like eviction defense, small claims, and uncontested divorces.

The work felt worthwhile, paid well, and I became part of the full time faculty – an associate professor on a tenure track. For the most part, I worked with students who wanted to learn the law to help people.

The director of the clinic was bright, funny and gregarious. He wanted everyone to enjoy the effort. An egalitarian, he found any excuse to spend school money mixing business with pleasure, and he always included the entire staff.

With my second marriage on the rocks, I met and fell in love with Kathy Cannon, a student director at CLAC. She was among the group that interviewed me for the job, confessing later that everyone on staff was afraid I might be too square for this wild office.

Apparently a suit, fresh haircut and some mouthwash made a difference.

Iran 1978

In late 1977, Iran started to change. In November, government agents attacked a not-so secret meeting of dissident intellectuals outside Tehran. A funeral for those killed, held by custom 40 days later, represented a protest. Thousands attended. They, too, were attacked by governmental forces. Another 40 days passed until a second funeral demonstration. More protestors and more people were killed, leading to yet another 40-day cycle. By the Spring of 1978, the Shah's regime began to appear vulnerable. What started as a solemn funeral protest for more democracy had evolved into an uprising.

Kathy and I had just started living together when my ISA friends, Zia and Reza, stopped by our apartment. They asked me to go to Iran again. I would have to leave within days, for an undetermined time.

My assignment would be different this time. Widespread unrest and open rebellion pushed the country toward a showdown, perhaps a revolution. June 5th would mark the 15th anniversary of the 1963 uprising that had seen 15,000 killed or imprisoned by the Shah's forces. In the immediate aftermath, Ayatollah Khomeini escaped into exile in Baghdad. He had been looking for a way to return ever since.

I felt I needed Kathy's approval to make this trip. She wasn't political. The importance of Iran and this moment, and the value of my involvement, might not register with her. It didn't help that I was unsure when I might return. Worse, I might get fired for leaving CLAC on such short notice.

She listened and tried to be supportive, but she couldn't guarantee she'd be there when I returned. I asked Zia and Reza to try to keep her on board, trusting and waiting for me. They agreed. Fingers crossed, I left L.A.

I checked into Hotel Elizabeth again. It had been less than three years since I first arrived in Tehran, but the capital now felt noticeably different. People seemed more open, talkative, fearless – a different city.

123

After the series of attacks, a palpable tension kept the city on edge. What might happen on the June 5th anniversary? Nobody knew what to expect. Everyone expected something big.

Most waited for guidance from Ayatollah Khomeini, now in exile in Paris. He finally issued a statement, calling for a "glorious silence." The reverse of an uprising, this was a call for people to stay at home, boycott, participate in a general strike. Other activists held a different view, preparing to take to the streets. The Shah's government threatened to respond with brutal force.

My main concern centered on lining up transportation for June 5th. I needed to get around, see whatever might be happening. I couldn't rely on the taxi system that day, so I tried to hire a taxi driver or free-lancer. Some turned me down. They weren't planning to work or go outside on June 5th. One driver wanted to observe the glorious silence. Another worried that "bullets might be flying."

I finally found a driver, and could only hope he'd come through. I would be extremely limited on foot. On the other hand, he might be a government agent.

Each morning newspaper chronicled the government's growing fear about June 5th. The Shah convened meetings of disparate groups: the national women's association, the labor federation, university professors. Each of these convocations was scheduled to end shortly before the anniversary. Each ended with a public statement applauding the Shah and calling for business-as-usual on June 5th.

Every day the front pages were filled with this propaganda and more. In response to unrest which had grown every month since November, the regime promised liberalization: people could exercise freedom of speech without fear of governmental retaliation or interference. The added proviso surprised no one: if protests turned into riots or disorder, governmental forces would react immediately and harshly.

My driver came through at the appointed place and time on the big day. He drove me all over. That turned out to be easy: the streets were empty, except military vehicles. Most shops and stores were closed. Tanks and soldiers took positions at big intersections. Tension was high, but nothing seemed to be happening – except the glorious silence.

The next day, I tried to find out if anything had gone down anywhere. The press claimed everything was wonderful. Locals disagreed. They were talkative. I got reports of an incident in a small town east of Isfahan, Iran's second largest city. The information sounded reliable. I flew to Isfahan on the next flight, then took a bus into town. By now – June 7th – no evidence of a public disturbance existed. No one would talk about events on the 5th. I couldn't find a westerner to talk to. No bars in town meant nowhere to find a westerner. I surrendered and flew back to Tehran the next day.

More days of frustration made it obvious there was nothing more for me to do. By now, Zia and Reza probably knew more about what happened in Iran on June 5 than I did. The whole flight back, I wondered if my new apartment in Hollywood would be empty.

Kathy was there! Zia and Reza stopped by to see her several times. Seasoned politicals, they patiently explained the basics of Marxism and imperialism, the particulars of Iran under the Shah as a puppet of the U.S. Kathy understood me now much better than before I left. We became politically simpatico. We married a year later.

Two months after I returned from Tehran, a fire at the Cinema Rex in Abadan, Iran, killed 422 people. They were trapped inside because all the doors were chained from the outside.

The Shah's regime and its mouthpieces blamed dissidents, linking the protests with mass murder and terrorism. The government's explanations sounded too readymade, too slick. The public refused to buy any of it. Most Iranians believed that SAVAK and the Shah were behind the massacre, and were trying to use the tragedy to stem the tide of rebellion. Khomeini blamed the regime. Public opinion embraced his view. For the Shah, it was now a matter of time.

Another LAPD Attack

The U.S. and other Western media repeated the official Iranian-U.S. narrative about the theater fire. The international ISA network began to demonstrate against this slanderous cover-up. On September 1st, a demonstration drew 400 people in L.A. This larger-than-usual turnout reflected the growing success of the anti-Shah movement in Iran and the U.S.

The march started at El Pueblo Plaza (Olvera Street) and stopped at the downtown federal building to note the U.S. role in the Shah's repression. Then we walked to the *L.A. Times* building, pausing on Broadway to signify the media's role in spreading propaganda that was sustaining the Shah's repressive regime.

Walking south toward Pershing Square, we encountered a line of police, suddenly appearing at the south end of the block (2nd St.). Cops with batons drawn corralled people against the west wall of the *Times* building, then formed a line surrounding all of us, effectively pinning us against that same wall. Why was a peaceful, lawful protest being pinned down by police in riot helmets and brandishing nightsticks?

Our group began to bulge like a bowl against the wall. The police line held three feet away from this curved mass of people. As a non-Iranian legal observer wearing a coat and tie, the cops let me come and go. I became the lone inhabitant of a no-man's land between the demonstrators and the shoulder-to-shoulder line of police, sealing us in.

Demonstrators knew me. The police accepted my presence. I asked the officer-in-charge to explain the reasoning of the police action, and how we could resolve this problem and all of us get on with our day.

I relayed messages between the police and the ISA leadership, who buried themselves within the crowd to make it difficult for the cops to get to them. These negotiations eased tensions. When not busy relaying messages, I paced that three-foot DMZ, keeping both sides separated, if only symbolically.

The stand-off lasted 15 minutes. I heard a collective breath come from the mass of people, which suddenly surged toward me and the cops with great force, completely breaking through the no man's land and police line, and causing pandemonium up and down the block.

Everyone everywhere shot into motion, scattering, stumbling, falling, getting up, running again. The police found themselves in similar disarray. Many were knocked down or spun around by the flood of escaping protestors. Swinging batons as a knee-jerk reaction, the police grabbed civilians as they darted by, wrestling many to the ground. I ducked to avoid being hit, and ran to avoid being tackled.

Within seconds, 100 had been forced face down in the street, bodies pointing in all directions. Purses, clothing and shoes – lots of shoes – littered the area. I would learn months later that a person's feet tend to shrink under stress. Shoes would often be the first casualties of that fight-or-flight reaction.

Three-quarters of the protestors, including the ISA leadership, escaped. After the chaotic, baton-swinging phase the police ignored me. I wandered openly in the field of battle, sidestepping cops and shoes, and people lying in the street. When the police began cuffing the detainees, I slowly walked away, making mental notes about any rough treatment. To my knowledge, no one was ever prosecuted as a result of this incident.

Meanwhile, the rebellion in Iran increased in the wake of the Cinema Rex theater fire. Martial law was declared. Workers in key industries went on strike. By autumn, it became clear that the tide had turned against the Shah. The media began reporting he was preparing to leave the country, looking for a safe place for exile. When rumors surfaced that he was seeking medical treatment in Panama, the ISA protested at the Panamanian Consulate.

Another rumor had him coming to Beverly Hills to stay with his sister. ISA and its L.A. allies staged a peaceful march to show that the Shah would not be welcome in Southern California.

During that demonstration, in February, 1979, a splinter group of students headed north toward the home of the Shah's sister. Police attempted to herd the small crowd back to the main demonstration. Out-running the police lines, protestors briefly rampaged through lush front yards.

Evening newscasts screamed about arson. Evidently, some bushes caught fire in the melee. A demonstration in this ritzy Beverly Hills neighborhood shocked police and the community. An outraged media painted the students as lawless terrorists. In response, ISA held a press conference at the L.A. Press Club. I was invited to sit at the speakers table. I didn't intend to say anything.

When media questions began sounding like attacks on the students, I grabbed the microphone and went on the offense. The demonstration came as an appropriate response to the threat of the Shah coming to town, I said. Exiled Iranians were rightfully outraged.

"What if Hitler wanted to move here?" I asked. "How would Beverly Hills react?"

My short, angry, and provocative comments received air time on more than one evening news program.

A few days later, the chairman of the tenure committee stepped into the elevator at the law school where I was teaching. He turned red and stammered at me. He lived in Beverly Hills. He had been outraged by my comments. To his mind, I had gone beyond academic freedom by condoning violence. A few months later, I was denied tenure. My teaching contract would not be renewed.

Shortly after the Beverly Hills incident, the Shah left Iran for exile in Egypt. Ayatollah Khomeini returned to Iran in triumph. The Pahlavi dynasty, viewed as a puppet of the U.S., was decisively dismantled.

Like so many other exiles worldwide, Zia and Reza returned to Iran after the 1979 revolution to help build a new, secular, democratic society that they believed Khomeini was promising. By 1981, however, Islamists had begun consolidating power. Those favoring democracy suffered pressure from an increasingly fundamentalist Khomeini and his Revolutionary Guard.

In January, 1982, Reza & Zia helped lead the Sarbedaran insurrection to take control of the northern town of Amol. As activists rallied the citizens, the Ayatollah's regime deployed ground and air forces, retaking the city after several days of fighting. Zia, Reza, and 19 other leaders were rounded up and jailed. On the one-year anniversary of the Amol uprising, all 21 were executed.

Zia and Reza remain two of the finest people I've ever known. Kathy and I both owe the success of our marriage partly to them. *Presente!*

The May Day Cases

When injustice becomes law, resistance becomes duty.
    — attributed to both THOMAS JEFFERSON and NELSON MANDELA

Some of those arrested in the Beverly Hills Hotel Iranian Student Association demonstration case in 1975 supported the Revolutionary Communist Party (RCP), which allied with ISA during those years. I started attending RCP demonstrations as a legal observer. I helped them get permits, handled a few criminal cases for them. Attending meetings and study groups, reading their newspaper (*Revolutionary Worker*, later renamed *Revolution*), I got more involved.

In mid-1979, RCP was planning a 1980 May Day celebration. Tensions between the U.S. and the Soviet Union threatened to come to a head in the 1980's. A third world war seemed possible, and uprisings in Central America and many other parts of the world gave hope for a new and better social order worldwide. Socialism and communism were strong political trends in the U.S. before WWII. The RCP hoped to re-establish May 1st as a day for working-class solidarity and militant struggle in the U.S. and around the world. This would help make revolution a visible alternative to perpetual economic crisis and war.

Still, I kept wondering how May Day '80 could be different from any other annual gathering of leftists waving red flags, giving speeches and singing *The Internationale*. Why all the nonstop articles and flyers for an event so many months away?

The plan started becoming clear to me in February, 1980, when a brigade of May Day volunteers arrived in L.A. to bolster local forces and guarantee making this May Day a big event. The brigade went to factories at shift change, when the night shift was walking to the parking lot, and the day shift was walking to the plant. Signs and flyers up, the volunteers tried to talk to workers about the need for a bold statement against the system of continuing war and economic crisis.

Not surprisingly, friction came from security guards and police. Neither had encountered this tactic at local factories in recent years. Arrests began the first day the brigade showed up. That had me scrambling to deal with bail, arraignments, and an influx of cases of minor crimes. I also went to factories in the early morning to help assert the brigade's right to use a public sidewalk, however unusual that may have seemed outside a factory, with little public foot traffic. Many in the brigade came from out of town and didn't have jobs, so it was harder to get low bail or "Own Recognizance" release. They all wanted to get out of jail and back on the streets ASAP. These experienced activists kept their mouths shut and waited patiently to get bailed out.

Police arrested brigade members in groups. They were arraigned in those same groups. Brigade members handed out flyers in the halls and made speeches in court before a judge took the bench. That produced a strain on the court system. At first the sheriff put extra bailiffs in the courtrooms. After a few of these tension-building episodes, I convinced some judges to let me represent brigade members, who knew me and trusted me. As their appointed legal counsel, I could minimize the chaos in the courthouse. And incidentally – I would get paid by the county!

Word spread. I was soon appointed on most every RCP case. I often suggested lawyers for the other defendants in multi-defendant cases, and they were often appointed. This aided the defendants who could then be excused from attending most court proceedings. After all, they really wanted to be out on the streets. Soon, they were.

The Will Rogers Park Case

On Saturday, April 5, 1980, I rode along on a 3/4-ton flatbed truck with the brigade through downtown L.A., waving signs, shouting, sometimes getting off the truck to hand out flyers, sell newspapers, and talk to people. A demonstration on wheels! As a legal observer, my job entailed talking to police, taking notes and recording names of witnesses. I dressed in a casual sport coat and loose tie – a lawyer overdressed for a sunny SoCal afternoon.

We made our way to Watts and a jazz festival in Will Rogers Park. The brigade started circulating among the crowds, holding signs, red flags, handing out flyers. Sheriff's cars pulled onto the grass near our flatbed. Deputies donned riot gear from their car trunks.

I tried to defuse the situation by walking up to a Sheriff who looked like he might be in charge. Introducing myself, I asked about the show of force, what brigade members might be doing wrong, what could be done to remedy that. I never got to finish that sentence.

The Sheriff grabbed my arm, spun me around, pushed my head and chest down on the hood of a patrol car. He cuffed my hands behind my back. With the side of my face pressed to the hood I could see deputies chasing my companions around the immediate area, swinging night sticks, grabbing and throwing brigade members to the ground, handcuffing them.

When the dust settled, nine men and five women had been arrested and taken to the notorious Firestone sheriff station in South Central L.A. Some arrestees had been hit, thrown to the ground, and injured during the arrests. We assessed the injuries as minor while sharing a holding cell. As we got booked – a matter-of-fact questioning by clerks: name, address, date of birth – a brigade member from Oakland named Riley kept complaining about pain. Surprisingly, guards removed him for medical attention. We would later find out he was an undercover cop. We never saw him again.

The arrested women were taken into a room across the hall from our booking cell. After a while, they were escorted out of that room and down the hall. The deputies appeared to be unnecessarily rough with the women, so some of us shouted at them to take it easy. The women disappeared down the hall. We started singing *The Internationale* to show solidarity. Minutes later, deputies massed outside our cell, opened the door, and started pulling us out and throwing us down the hall in a gauntlet worthy of a drunken fraternity initiation.

I was the first one they grabbed. They pulled me out of the cell and tossed me against the wall. I managed to get my hands out in front of me to stop my face from slamming into the wall. Then I was hustled down a hall lined with deputies who were striking at me with batons. The final deputy in the gauntlet shoved me against an iron door at the end of the hall. That door opened. Someone threw me into a cell of iron bars. Dazed, I eyed a door to my right and made a run for the safety of our destination – the large holding cell in front of me.

Two young black men were sitting on the floor, somewhat startled to see a white man thrown around like that, then another, and another, until the eight of us (not all white) were locked inside. I took at least one hard baton blow to the back, but was not hurt. Others weren't so lucky. Some hit the wall, iron door, or bars with their face, and were bleeding. Others were hit or kicked and now in obvious pain.

The moment the cell door was click shut, an arm with a can of pepper spray doused the cell. Some of us hadn't yet caught our breath. Our coughing, wheezing, and moaning finally died down. One of the black men asked, "What the hell did you guys do?"

An hour later we got loaded onto a bus with other prisoners and driven to Men's Central Jail downtown. The booking process seemed to take forever. We had to strip and get sprayed with a delousing agent. After a shower, we slipped into worn-but-clean orange jump suits.

I had been inside "county" many times as an attorney, but only in one of the visiting areas. This was my first view from the inside.

The relatively modern, sterile and over-lit jail had inside observation booths. We walked single-file down wide, yellow concrete block halls, keeping to the far right with our eyes on the floor. Because I had a working relationship with a resourceful bail bondswoman, I made bail after a long night. I walked out of "county" at 6 a.m., Easter morning. The sun was just starting to rise.

That morning began the four-year odyssey of fighting an absurd nightmare of criminal charges. On one hand, all 13 of us were booked on charges of battery against peace officers, plus inciting a riot and other serious charges arising from a documented violent mass arrest. Police reports made us sound like terrible criminals, although a bit cartoonish.

On the other hand, the District Attorney only filed misdemeanors – not felonies. These lower charges were also filed in a small, out-of-the-way municipal court, not in Superior Court. This came as a huge relief. Our liability maxed-out at one year in county jail on each count, instead of several years in prison.

The misdemeanor charges did something else for us. They sent a signal to the judge that something was wrong with the case. It made no sense to allege serious crimes in the arrest reports, then file puny misdemeanor charges in court. Was the arrest report a fantasy?

That report claimed the brigade caused a major disturbance in the park, that I gave a soapbox speech calling on the people to "rise up and kill the pigs." On the basis of this allegation, I was booked for threatening death or great bodily injury to a police officer. My bail was set higher than the other arrestees. But this charge was never filed by the D.A. Apparently, prosecutors had little faith in the truth of the police report.

And the brigade didn't have time to disturb the peace. Deputies rolled up as soon as we off-loaded. RCP had no intention to disturb the peace anyway. And I didn't have any time to find a soapbox to give any speech, either. I walked straight from the flatbed to the deputy in charge. And as a legal observer, political speeches were not in my job description.

If I had given a speech, I wouldn't say anything so ridiculous to anyone – certainly not to black people in Watts. That allegation against me was so ridiculous I think it helped us by casting doubt on the whole the police report.

That report also alleged that I started the scuffle in the county jail. According to the report, we were making a commotion, causing a lone jailer to open the cell door in order to take some of us to another cell. When he opened the cell door, the report claimed, I supposedly grabbed the jailer's arm and pulled him inside, whereupon we all started hitting and kicking this helpless man. The fraudulent spirit of that official account became transparent: no photos of the jailer's injuries could be produced. No medical report on him had ever been filed. A jailer pulled into cell and beaten by eight men, yet not a single photo showing any injury, and no medical report to substantiate the story. Credible? No way.

What we called The Will Rogers Park Case dragged on for four years. It never went to trial. Eventually, the entire case was dismissed.

One highlight of this bizarre case came in court when all 13 of us arrived for our first appearance. The South Gate Municipal Court – a one-story courthouse with two small courtrooms – was ill-equipped to handle a case with so many defendants and an equal number of lawyers. (I represented myself.)

Most of the defendants were unemployed activists who could not afford a lawyer. Each was entitled to a court-appointed lawyer. A friend and law school classmate, Robert Mann, agreed to serve as lead counsel. Kathy knew lawyers who took court-appointed criminal cases. We assembled a friendly, cooperative group.

By this time, judges were advised to let me suggest lawyers. Courts had been accepting my suggestions. Peaceful court appearances, not chaos, resulted from this process. And fine criminal lawyers worked on our cases, getting paid by the county. But this would be different. In this case, I was also a defendant.

South Gate judge Frank Gafkowski seemed afraid of us at first. Additional bailiffs were brought into court. After the first few appearances, the judge ruled that defendants would not have to show up. There wasn't much room for them, and the court didn't really want them.

Judge Gafkowski also felt obliged to explain things to the defendants. That took more of the court's time. Without the defendants present, court appearances became a little like class reunions of a dozen lawyers.

At first the judge wouldn't permit me in his chambers with the other lawyers. I was a defendant, and he didn't know me. He was forced to deal with me, however, because I served as my own counsel. He attempted to talk to me only in open court and on the record. That unusual situation quickly became difficult. Most of the actual court business would take place in chambers.

As soon as the judge confirmed that I was regarded as a good guy in the criminal defense community – and probably harmless in any event – I was permitted into his chambers. Judge Gafkowski and I would soon sit at the same table at a Criminal Courts Bar Association dinner. We got along fine that night. Of course, we couldn't discuss the case.

This case dragged on for so many years because we took two pre-trial writs up to the court of appeals, and each took many months. We pursued every angle in getting every bit of evidence that might be helpful. Nobody was in a hurry. Defendants were out going about their lives, and neither the D.A. nor the judge had any enthusiasm for the case. Robert Mann did all the work and stood in for the other lawyers in court those few times when he and I had to show up for something.

During pre-trial hearings we discovered that the LAPD red squad (Public Disorder Intelligence Division) had been following our flatbed truck all day, taking photos, keeping tabs on us, making radio reports to their supervisors, and to other units and agencies. It became clear that the Sheriff – prompted by LAPD – decided in advance to swoop down and arrest us all in Will Rogers County Park. What we did would not have mattered. That would explain why deputies were able to drive onto the grass en-masse the moment we began to offload.

Armed with a solid theory of the case, we went for the jugular. We subpoenaed radio calls, supervisor logs, inter-agency memos. We took the Sheriff and the LAPD to court when they didn't give us documents we were entitled to. We filed appeals when the judge denied any important request. Motion work is paper work. Robert handled most of that.

He also filed a civil suit on our behalf, for false arrest, use of unnecessary force, and civil rights violations. The information we forced production of in the criminal case would be very helpful in the civil case. But we put the civil action on hold until the criminal case was over, which was a long time. In 1984, both sides agreed to file mutual dismissals. The overblown misdemeanor case against us died quietly without ever going to trial.

I would clash with Steve Weiss, the deputy D.A. assigned to RCP cases, many times in the early '80's, in several courts around L.A. County. On two occasions during the four years of The Will Rogers Park case, Steve recommended that all charges be dropped. Both times his recommendation made to District Attorney Ira Reiner, who said no.

But the case was finally dismissed, and for the first time in four years I had no criminal charges pending against me.

Other Cases

Not to be left out, the L.A. City Attorney brought a misdemeanor case against me in 1980.

That February, I assisted a rolling flatbed truck demonstration in downtown L.A. A cop directed the driver to go straight for two blocks, then turn right and pull over. I jumped on the running board. The driver told me he feared the police might attack or arrest us on that isolated street. He turned right on the first street – busier and therefore safer for us – and pulled to the curb. The angry cop wrote a ticket for the reason he pulled us over for in the first place. Still upset, the cop chewed me out, taking my name and address.

A few weeks, later, I received a letter from the City Attorney. I had been charged with the crime of obstructing an officer in the performance of his duties. I would have to appear in court for arraignment.

The ACLU could represent me this time. My alleged crime was pure speech – talking to the driver. The ACLU refused to represent me in the Will Rogers Park case because violence had been alleged in the police report.

A bright, enthusiastic young lawyer – Rees Lloyd – was assigned to my case. He did a first-rate job, making motions that raised creative legal issues and appearing in court many times over the course of a year. The case was assigned to the misdemeanor courts downtown, where I knew judges and lawyers and where I continued to handle cases almost every day. I attended the hearings on my case whenever able, in part just to freak everyone out. One judge joked: "Mr. Eiden, are you here today as a lawyer, a defendant – or both?"

Rees argued that the charge against me was vague. How could we adequately defend the case without knowing exactly what I was supposed to have done? Obstructing an officer? How had I done that? The police report had not mentioned that detail.

The judge rewarded my lawyer's persistence by ordering the prosecutor to amend the complaint to include exactly how I had allegedly obstructed the officer. In a few weeks we received the amended complaint. I was accused of "aiding and abetting an illegal right turn." The case was set for trial after a year of intense legal wrangling by a dogged and diligent defense lawyer.

On the day of trial, the City Attorney dismissed the case without giving a reason, other than the catch-all "in the interest of justice." Rees believed the prosecutors would look foolish trying to convince a jury to convict me of what did not appear to be a real crime. It sounded more like a late-night talk show joke. Another significant problem: no evidence existed of what I supposedly told the driver. For all anyone knew, I had advised him to follow the officer's instructions. The case was so absurd, it was a wonder prosecutors litigated it for a year – a lot of work for them and for my ACLU lawyer.

All in all, RCP supporters accounted for some 300 arrests in the L.A. area from 1980 to 1983, mostly misdemeanor trespassing, disturbing the peace, resisting arrest, obstructing an officer, and battery on an officer. In most cases police overreacted and harassed, arrested, and even attacked people who were finding effective ways to influence public opinion legally. Brigade members didn't want to get arrested or killed, but they were dedicated and ready for anything. Indeed, brigade member Damien Garcia, a Will Rogers Park defendant, was stabbed to death on April 22 while leading a small, otherwise peaceful march through Pico Gardens, a housing project just east of downtown L.A. I tried to keep track of all the arrests, bail and cases, and I worked with other lawyers and assistants to make sure all aspects were being dealt with adequately.

Some cases were more important than others. Felony charges were a high priority, of course. So were misdemeanor cases involving multiple defendants and/or important defendants. Politically more important incidents, serious violations of rights, and brutality also affected the level of significance.

Most arrests involved the overreaction by a cop or security guard. In some cases, these officials were trying to put a stop to activities that annoyed them or seemed unusual or out of place – but not illegal. When a police officer would say, "Stop," my clients would say "No, we have a right to be here doing this." Sometimes an official would back down, but sometimes an incident would ensue and arrests would be made. Sometimes the prosecutor questioned the worthiness of filing charges. More likely, charges got filed.

I tried to be creative by filing more pre-trial motions than most criminal defense lawyers. Misdemeanor courts weren't accustomed to pretrial motions in minor cases. We usually reviewed the disciplinary records of the guards or officers involved, hunting for previous misconduct, possible prejudice, or connections to the red squad. Our May Day cases helped uncover wrongdoing by LAPD's Public Disorder Intelligence Division (PDID), and contributed to a scandal that caused the dissolution of PDID. Cynics would claim the unit was simply moved to another floor and renamed the Anti-Terrorist Division – ATD.

We also requested documents the police and prosecutors would not normally turn over in misdemeanor cases. In essence, we did our best to make ourselves pains in the ass. As a result, many cases were dismissed before trial.

My favorite weapon was finding a way to put the prosecution on defense, to get them and the police to reveal things they didn't normally disclose and didn't want to reveal. I called it "getting into their shorts," and it started with a thorough discovery motion. Our experience with police cases helped us figure out what evidence we could expect to be generated in any particular case. My cynicism about police and prosecutors sometimes helped prove they were withholding evidence. I was always suspicious and always dug for it.

I requested a long list of specific items, and the more the judge ordered prosecutors to produce, the more potential leverage I achieved. If the judge refused to grant an important or obvious item, I would take a writ to a higher court.

I routinely made motions with little chance of winning. More than once some other lawyer said my motion didn't have a chance, that I was wasting my time and "the courts time"

I would answer, "OK, tell me my chances, percentage wise."

He might shrug his shoulders. I'd jump in: "How about five percent? Think that's a fair estimate – twenty to one?"

"That sounds about right."

"So that means," I'd say, "when I run a motion like this twenty times, I'll win one case that you won't win."

I learned a lot from these motions. I gained leverage when any prosecutor had a hard time finding the information ordered. Another reason for running these "loser" motions was to remind the criminal justice system of its own arbitrary nature. I strived to make police repeat, explain and defend a lie. I searched for conflicts of interest and other chinks in the prosecutorial armor.

On one hand, prosecutors and judges usually didn't like handling our cases and wanted us out of their lives. On the other hand, these cases often provided some drama in court jobs which could be routine and boring. Some of our long, multi-defendant misdemeanor cases were sent to the civil courthouse where judges could spend more time dealing with a complex case. The criminal courts experienced very high volume in those days.

The criminal justice system began to adjust to President Reagan's war on drugs. Millions of black men were now going through the system to prisons. In the next three decades, "mass incarceration," as defined by legal scholar and civil rights litigator Michelle Alexander in *The New Jim Crow* (The New Press: 2010), became the accepted norm.

Throughout the '80s, jails, courts, prisons, and probation and parole departments stayed busy processing drug defendants. Courthouse halls backed up with black men and their families waiting to go into a courtroom. Lockups filled with black men unable to make bail. Everybody noticed the alarming percentage of black defendants, but everyone came up with a different explanation, and no one knew what to do. Some citizens didn't care, of course. It was none of their business. Besides, nothing could be done. This was just how the justice system was working now.

It was clearly a broken system.

One of our large cases with pretrial motions was sent to an eviction court. There, we offered a refreshing change from standard landlord-tenant disputes. Judge Ernest Aubrey found free speech and similar issues, both important and interesting, even in misdemeanor cases. Thoughtful and attentive, Judge Aubrey believed every case deserved justice. He allowed adequate time to prepare and to argue motions, present evidence. His decisions stood as some of the most scholarly and balanced I had seen or heard at any level.

One of our May Day cases started with two people handing out flyers and talking to students in a grassy area of a local community college during the noon hour. They were told by campus police that a permit was needed. Our clients knew their rights. They weren't littering, breaking any laws or bothering anybody. That was not what the police wanted to hear. They expected people to do what they were told.

Our clients continued leafleting. Campus police arrested them for disturbing the peace. This actually came as a relief. Cops routinely alleged resistance, adding charges of resisting arrest and/or battery on an officer. That would up the ante and make a plea bargain more difficult to refuse.

I represented a female defendant, Carol, in that case. Tom Case, a Compton public defender, represented her partner.

The arresting officer testified that both defendants were shouting, thereby disturbing classes in progress: "They were yelling so loud I could hear them".

Tom asked him, "How far away were you?"

After some thought, the officer said, "About seventy-five feet."

"So it's your testimony," Tom asked, "that someone talking loud enough to be heard 75 feet away is disturbing the peace of a college campus?"

The officer replied, "Yes, sir".

Glancing around the courtroom, Tom walked down the aisle halfway to the back of the room, turned around and in a calm, conversational tone of voice asked the officer, "Can you hear me?"

The courtroom stood quiet. The answer was obvious. Everyone in the room had heard him clearly. Then Tom walked past the last row of seats to the farthest corner from the witness stand and asked, in the same conversational tone of voice, "Can you hear me now?"

Again the answer was obvious. Tom lowered his voice almost to a whisper. "Can you hear me now?"

Everyone in the courtroom could hear him, though barely.

This remains one of the most stunning courtroom moments I have ever witnessed. The truth had become immediately obvious to everyone.

Many judges have diagrams of their courts for this purpose, so when Tom asked for the record, how far the far corner stood from the witness stand, the judge produced the room diagram and noted, "Fifty-seven feet."

Tom won our case with those questions and his final argument:

"You heard the evidence. Merely speaking loud enough to be heard seventy-five feet away cannot constitute the crime of disturbing the peace of a college campus."

I then argued that no teacher or student had testified that his or her peace had been disturbed by our clients. The jury agreed and quickly found both defendants not guilty. Carol would become a key person in the El Salvador Tour Case the following year.

We won almost all our cases that went to trial in those years. In one felony case, the May Day Brigade was attacked while demonstrating at an older home in Hollywood, one being used as an immigration (INS) detention facility.

A few dozen people picketed on the sidewalk in front of that house. The LAPD Hollywood Division sent a large contingent of police, who charged out of their cars and immediately arrested several people. Five were charged with 11 felonies, most involving battery on a police officer. The protesters were never asked to stop picketing. No police officer advised any of them to leave. The responding cops simply arrested anyone they could grab. And once again, no underlying crime was charged, which belies the alleged need to grab these folks.

The trial of this felony case took almost a month. Similar numbers of witnesses on both sides took the stand. With all those witnesses, five defendants, and 11 felony counts to consider, the jury was out for three weeks. It stands as the longest deliberation I have ever encountered.

In long trials with multiple counts, the court would typically allow lawyers to go about their business while the jury deliberated. Lawyers were expected to stay in telephone contact with the court clerk, so for the first few days of jury deliberation in this case, I kept the clerk informed of my whereabouts, calling in every hour. The following week, I checked in less frequently. By the third week, I carried on my practice as though I'd forgotten this jury was still out.

We never even heard from the jury during its deliberations – also highly unusual. Juries normally have questions or issues every day, and that meant all the parties would be called back to court.

I wasn't the only one who forgot about the jury. It took a while to get us all back for the verdict. Under the circumstances, the court was understanding.

Three defendants were acquitted completely. Two were convicted of misdemeanor ("lesser included") counts, not the charged felonies. Eleven felony charges had wound up as three misdemeanors. Two defendants received probation, no fine, no more jail.

On one hand, this represented a positive outcome for a felony case. On the other hand, it stood as one of the worst outcomes of all 300 May Day arrests in Los Angeles during those three years, again proving that there was little or nothing illegal going on when the cops decided to take action, or if there was, it wasn't important enough to charge.

145

There were several plea bargains in our May Day cases over this time frame, especially small cases in remote courts, like San Diego, where we didn't want to go to trial, and didn't even want to make the long drive south for one more court appearance.

Most of those defendants were not local folks. They were unlikely to get in trouble in the area again, so pleading to a misdemeanor and getting summary probation didn't seem unreasonable or unjust. Still, we hated those plea bargains and tried our best to avoid them.

All in all I spent about six years on RCP cases generated between 1980 and 1983. I did most of this work *pro bono*, but did get paid for court-appointed cases. In those days, courts didn't strictly limit the bills lawyers submitted. $50 an hour was the standard rate for misdemeanors. I could expect to be paid for every hour I billed. This meant I could devote as much time as needed – a luxury for a criminal defense lawyer serving poor activists.

V

THE
EL SALVADOR
TOUR CASE

Truth is the first casualty of war.
— AESCHYLUS (circa 460 BCE)

Wake Up Call

One morning in October, 1981, Carol called and told me that she and three men had been arrested. They needed me to bail them out. This didn't come as the biggest surprise in the world. I started asking the usual questions:

"Where are you? What jail? What agency arrested you. For what?"

It did come as a big surprise when she said, "We're someplace called Miami, Oklahoma. In an INS jail. It's a long story."

Where the hell was Miami, Oklahoma? And what was an INS jail doing there? Carol didn't have time to answer questions. She didn't want to say much over the phone anyway, especially on a jail phone.

I made a few calls, packed light. Kathy drove me to LAX for a red-eye to Tulsa, the nearest airport to Miami, OK.

I assumed I would just bail them out and be back in three or four days, a week at most. It didn't work out that way.

Carol had been driving with David, Emilio, and Lucas, en route to begin a speaking tour about the civil wars then raging in El Salvador and other Central American countries. David and Emilio, refugees from El Salvador, had seen their lives threatened for opposing the brutal U.S.-sponsored regime.

Knowing the risks of speaking out against the government, even here in free-speech USA, they remained anxious to tell Americans about the political repression in their home country – and to describe the U.S. role in it.

They offered personal testimony that our government was lying about the corrupt, death squad regimes the U.S. supported in Central America. The extent of that support would also surprise everyone who listened. And all the while, the media repeated the government propaganda.

Eighteen months earlier, El Salvador's fourth Archbishop, Óscar Arnulfo Romero y Galdámez, was assassinated at the altar during Mass. Romero spoke out on behalf of the poor, condemning the brutal conditions and the violent acts inflicted upon those who tried to change the vicious, unjust system.

Before his murder, Archbishop Romero gained international attention in weekly articles and his popular radio show. He regularly informed his country of attacks and outrages that had gone unreported. More than 50 priests and nuns had been attacked in the past six years. Six were killed. Others were beaten, tortured, detained, or thrown out of the country. Churches and off-campus church facilities were fire bombed.

The Archbishop often made the point that the church itself was under attack. It stood for "the least of these" against a landowning class that resembled a feudal state. Romero himself remained safe until he started speaking out. Once he did, most priests and activists still continued to play it safe, keeping quiet about the indignities and horrors suffered by the peasants.

In his weekly sermon the day before his death, Romero called on Salvadoran soldiers as Christians to obey God's higher law and stop carrying out the government's repression of the poor and the church. The next morning, Monday, March 24, 1980, as he stood at the altar in the Chapel of Providence cancer hospital, a lone assassin emerged from a red car, walked in and shot Romero through the heart. The assailant, believed to have been sponsored by a death-squad leader, then returned to his car and drove away.

A week later, 250,000 mourners from around the world attended his funeral mass. The Pope sent a personal representative to the service.

Jesuit priest and Catholic pacifist John Dear said Romero's funeral was the largest demonstration in Salvadoran history – perhaps in the history of Latin America.

In death-squad El Salvador, no place or event could be considered truly safe. Smoke bombs exploded on the street in front of the Metropolitan Cathedral during the funeral service. Shots rang out. A stampede ensued. Before order was restored, 31 people were officially listed as casualties. Journalists at the scene reported a higher total – more than 50. As the gunfire continued, Romero's body was placed in a crypt beneath the sanctuary.

This violence took place while the eyes of the world focused on a huge international event. Far worse violence was believed to be taking place while the world wasn't watching.

El Salvador's primary international airport now bears Romero's name. He was beatified in May, 2014 by Pope Francis, who called the new saint "a voice that continues to resonate."

Major events, like Archbishop Romero's assassination and funeral, proved to be the only way the U.S. public learned anything about conditions in Central America. The Salvador Tour that Carol organized intended to break the information blackout on uprisings and death squads, and the tactic backing some regimes received from the U.S.

With the tour scheduled to start in Chicago, the four had been driving day and night from L.A. They arrived at a toll booth in the northeast corner of Oklahoma, very near the Missouri state line. Little did they know that the INS had an office nearby and regularly checked busses and cars headed to St. Louis and beyond.

David – who did not speak English – was driving, with Emilio asleep in the front seat as their blue Chevy station wagon rolled up to the toll plaza at 4 a.m. Both English speakers, Carol and Lucas, slept in the backseat. The toll operator saw brown faces, heard Spanish from the driver, called Border Patrol agents over.

All four in the station wagon were arrested and taken to the INS office and jail in nearby Miami. Carol and Lucas – U.S. citizens – were charged with federal felonies and moved to federal jail in Tulsa. The car, messy from the four-day drive, was impounded as evidence.

David and Emilio were charged in federal court with misdemeanor immigration crimes. Their bail was set low.

They were also charged by INS with being in the U.S. illegally, and subject to the deportation process in INS courts. For that reason, they would remain in the INS jail in Miami.

An activist from Chile, Lucas grew up in the U.S. His mother was also an outspoken activist. Lucas served as interpreter for David and Emilio at speaking engagements. Carol functioned as the tour organizer. She and Lucas now faced up to five years on each of two felony counts: transporting illegal aliens. Their bail was set much higher.

It took longer to bail them out than the three days I anticipated. A defense committee was hastily formed in L.A. to raise money and awareness, especially in places where the El Salvador Tour was scheduled to make presentations.

The committee used our house in Silverlake as an office and meeting place. People came and went in and out of the house at all hours. Kathy became deeply involved in the work.

News about The El Salvador Tour Case appeared in articles of college and leftist newspapers. Leaflets circulated on campuses and other key locations, like Telegraph Ave in Berkeley. In no time, the case became a tool for informing people about events in El Salvador. The overall response was positive.

I found a room in a one-story roadside motel on the main highway through Miami, allowing me to visit David and Emilio every day – sometimes twice a day – until they were freed on bail.

I also drove to Tulsa to see Carol and Lucas in federal jail several times. Bad things were sometimes known to happen to political activists while in custody, so I wanted to remind authorities that my clients were being looked after.

However, my primary concern centered on David and Emilio. They were especially vulnerable to intimidation, threats, and abuse. Worst case: they might be forced or talked into signing a voluntary departure declaration. If that happened, they would and be on their way back to El Salvador by morning, facing dire consequences.

I spent a lot of time on the phone that week, mostly talking to committee people about money, finding a bail bondsperson in Tulsa, talking to other lawyers, court clerks and jailers. I bailed out David and Emilio in six days. Lucas and Carol would take more time.

Carol made the decisions in this group. She chose to let the other three out first. In court in Tulsa, I managed to get bail lowered for her and Lucas. Still, it would take another week before both of them walked out of federal jail.

By that time, it became clear that I wouldn't be going home any time soon. The two misdemeanor and two felony cases were not going away. I knew no lawyer in the area who could be trusted to fight the case properly for a fee we could afford. The end of October was fast approaching. I asked Kathy to send me more clothes.

In the meantime, the committee in L.A. feared that the four might be targeted further by government agencies or vigilantes, and was anxious to get them out of Oklahoma ASAP. Their lawyer – me – had to accompany them, so as soon as Carol and Lucas were finally out of jail, the five of us drove north on I-44 to St. Louis – the new first stop on The Tour.

We stayed for a few days, unwinding with generous and supportive local activists who lived in a large Victorian house. They hosted a casual pot-luck for activists and Central American immigrants – and for the four revolutionaries just released from jail. In that joyous evening, we all celebrated having escaped from the clutches of The Man.

At The Tour's first public event the next night, David and Emilio finally got a chance to recount the nightmare taking place in their homeland, and about the complicity of the U.S. This would be their first experience working with an interpreter and answering questions from a university audience. Lucas discovered that interpreting wasn't easy, no matter how fluent he might be in two languages.

It was both a learning experience and a great evening!

152

Tulsa

After a few restful days in St. Louis, Carol and I were dropped off at the airport. The El Salvador Tour drove on to Chicago with a new coordinator.

Back to Tulsa, Carol and I started preparing a legal defense. I had worked with Carol on cases in Los Angeles, including cases in which she was a defendant. I knew her as consistent, thoughtful, and on task. A serious Marxist, she rejected the traditional role of the passive defendant who deferred to professionals and to the system. She had contempt for the "Halls of Justice," especially the prosecutorial and police components, which she regarded as enforcement arms of a corrupt political system.

Carol always insisted on talking things through thoroughly in order to understand and anticipate every possible problem or turn of events. She struggled patiently, but persistently, with my professional training and perspective. I evaluated criminal charges more narrowly, with an eye to finding angles that would lead to beating the charges. She reminded me that in addition to winning and staying out of prison, she stood shoulder-to-shoulder with dedicated political activists who wanted to provide a larger context in court, exposing a jury to the full, authentic story.

This meant revealing as much as possible about the murderous and hypocritical role of our own government in the bloody civil wars raging throughout Central America. If U.S. government surrogates actually kidnapped and murdered the opposition in El Salvador, including Archbishop Romero, then what might they do to silence their enemies? If a jury was left with with only a legal question – had Carol and Lucas known that David and Emilio were in the U.S. illegally? – a conviction seemed inevitable. We needed to create handholds for the jury to acquit.

Serious help came in the form of a lawyer and a paralegal from Houston. Glen Van Slyke and Mara Youngdahl spent much of November and December sharing the house and the legal work with us. I met and worked with Glen three years earlier while representing the Iranian Students

153

Association. I stayed with him in Houston once on a stop in my tour of speaking engagements about my trips to Iran.

Glen and Mara were well-known Texas radicals. Glen had been denied admission to the Texas State Bar because of an arrest at an anti-war demonstration in college years earlier. In return, he waged a lengthy public lawsuit to become admitted to practice law.

Mara had some legal knowledge and experience as the daughter of a famous leftist lawyer. She was also one of the Moody Park Three, indicted in Houston for inciting Houston's Moody Park rebellion-riot in 1978. That event would prove to be the match that lit the dry kindling of historic abuse by the white power structure in Houston.

Off-duty Houston police officers had arrested a 23-year old Vietnam Vet, Jose Campos Torres, in early May, 1977, on charges of disorderly conduct in a bar in the Mexican-American East End neighborhood. Brutally beaten, Torres was in such bad shape that the local jail refused to book him and ordered that he be taken to a hospital. The arresting officers did not comply with that instruction. Three days later – Mother's Day – Torres' body was found in Buffalo Bayou, a creek near the city's downtown area, the same place police had earlier beaten him bloody and senseless.

Former Houston Police Chief Harry Robinson called the crime "the greatest miscarriage of public trust by police officers in my 27 years of wearing a badge."[1]

Murder charges were filed against two police officers. They were convicted of negligent homicide, received probation and a $1 fine. Three other police officers, convicted on federal civil rights violations, each served nine months in prison.

These light sentences mocked the brutal murder of a young Vietnam Vet. To many in Houston, this favored treatment represented decades of oppression, including *No dogs or Mexicans allowed* signs – routinely enforced by local police.

On the one-year anniversary of Torres' death, 40 people were arrested in Moody Park for arson, assault, battery, and resisting arrest. Days later, Mara and her two compatriots were arrested, charged simply with conspiracy to riot: nine

154

counts against each, representing a collective potential of 140 years in prison. No overt acts were alleged.

So Mara was coming to us fresh off winning an intense legal and political battle. She didn't mind getting away from Houston for a while.

By the beginning of November, Carol had located a free house for us to live in and use as an office. The neighborhood dated to the 1920's, rebuilt after the 1921 riots, when white Tulsans rampaged, murdered, and burned down the prosperous Greenwood business district and its adjoining black community. The attack on Greenwood included fire bombs dropped from airplanes – something never before experienced. More than 300 people were brutally murdered, some in their own homes.

Our small frame house had electricity, a few pieces of furniture. The kitchen had a gas stove and fridge. The only bedroom held one bed. A couch, TV, and a wood-burning stove stood in the living room. No gas or electric heat, no running water. We brought in jugs of water to be used for everything from cooking to washing our hands and brushing our teeth. We flushed the toilet by dumping a half bucket of water straight down the middle with a little force.

The house had been a restaurant in earlier years. Families of mice had moved in. I got the job of in-house exterminator. Soon, I was catching a half-dozen mice a day. Then the weather turned cold. By mid-December, the rodents disappeared. Being a Southern Californian, I suddenly empathized with those mice. I had no experience with cold like this. Kathy sent a box of my heaviest clothes, boots, jackets, long-johns, gloves, and winter hats. I usually only wore this stuff when visiting the mountains.

Three of us – Carol, me and the new El Salvador Tour coordinator, Betsy – slept in separate areas near the pot-bellied stove, hanging a blanket over the kitchen doorway to keep heat from escaping. One day, I made goulash with noodles, ground beef, corn, tomatoes, and onions. After dinner, I left the large, half-full pot on the stove. The next morning, we discovered the leftovers frozen solid.

Glen and Mara slept in the bedroom, with no heat. That room was usually below freezing each night. They had sleeping bags, privacy, and each other. They also drove home to their cozy beds in Houston a few times, especially over the holidays. The rest of us were trapped in Tulsa.

I spent most of November and December at Tulsa University Law School library. One of our group drove me there early each morning and we usually stopped at the local Quick Trip for a 10-cent cup of coffee. Early on I went to the men's gym on campus and explained that I was in town for a few weeks, working in the law library most every day, and would greatly appreciate gym privileges and the use of a locker. They were very kind and welcoming and I worked out and showered there most every morning before getting started in the library.

After a short lunch break, I'd work at the Law Library until dinner time. Often, I'd go to the Library Restaurant off campus on 11th street for early-bird dinners. I loved to play *The Logical Song,* by Supertramp, on their jukebox. The cashier punched my card: buy 10 dinners and get one free. Ten more would qualify me for a tee shirt emblazoned with *The Library Restaurant, Tulsa Oklahoma.*

I wore that souvenir for years.

The staff of the law library had only two typewriters available to the public. They let me take over one of them for hours at a time.

With so many reference volumes at my disposal, so much table space to spread out the research, plus a typewriter and blank paper, I was practicing guerrilla law on the cheap. No great legal scholar, I threw myself into research, creative legal writing and strategy. Being stuck in Tulsa with nothing else to do turned out to be an education.

The Case

David and Emilio's only crime was not having immigration papers in their possession. How could they be required to carry documents they had never been issued? If this was the true intent of the law, hundreds of thousands each year could be charged with the same crime.

My research discovered that only eight people had ever been prosecuted since this law was enacted in 1934. This bolstered our argument that The Tour was being selectively prosecuted in order to silence its message – that the U.S. supported death-squad democracy in Central America. David and Emilio had been charged pricipally to pressure them to testify against Carol and Lucas.

Armed with this logic and the statistics supporting it, we made a motion to dismiss the charges, based on discriminatory prosecution. Other motions claimed the charge made no sense, contradicted the deportation charge, and was factually impossible. The INS charged David and Emilio with having no immigration papers, so how could the U.S. Attorney charge them with crimes for not possessing those papers?

On December 10, Judge Brett dismissed the misdemeanor cases on the grounds that no one could be prosecuted for failing to do something which was impossible for him to do. The decision was published at 528 F. Supp. 972 (1981).

The dismissal lifted a huge weight off our shoulders! The felony trial of Carol and Lucas had been set for January 4. We were facing the daunting prospect of two trials in three weeks. Now, jail, probation, and criminal records no longer hung over the heads of David and Emilio. Criminal convictions would have barred them from refugee status. As proud revolutionaries, they might be targets in jail or prison. Bad things could happen to people in jail, especially those the system didn't like.

Although criminal charges had been dismissed, David and Emilio still faced immigration proceedings and possible deportation to El Salvador – another place bad things kept happening to opponents of the regime.

In the felony case against Lucas and Carol, we filed a fat *omnibus* motion attacking the complaint from several angles and seeking dismissal of the charges. We emphasized discriminatory prosecution and tried to disclose communications between the arresting agency (INS Border Patrol) and other agencies, especially the FBI and the LAPD red squad (PDID: Public Disorder Intelligence Division), which probably knew about The Tour before it left Los Angeles. Unfortunately, we had neither time nor resources to litigate pre-trial discovery motions – the tactic I had used successfully in L.A. The judge made it clear that the trial would start on January 4, whether we were ready or not.

Carol and Lucas had been charged with transporting illegal immigrants. That required proof of criminal intent. In this case, that meant knowing that David and Emilio were in the U.S. illegally. One motion to dismiss came on the ground that Carol and Lucas had a good faith belief that David and Emilio were legitimate political refugees. This motion proved to be the key to our eventual victory.

As expected, the judge refused to grant our motion to dismiss. He did, however, rule that the jury could decide whether the defendants had criminal knowledge of David and Emilio's immigration status. We could now introduce relevant evidence of political repression in El Salvador as circumstantial evidence to support their eligibility for political asylum. We could substantiate U.S. complicity in that repression, the silencing of opposing views, and the fact that refugee status was being routinely granted or denied by the U.S. based on politics, not merit. By presenting this evidence, I could argue Lucas and Carol had reason to believe that David and Emilio were legitimate political refugees under U.S. immigration law.

Judge Thomas Brett followed the rules. Like most judges, he wanted to appear decisive, even rigid. At first he imposed a local rule: out-of-state lawyers needed local counsel on the case. We asked around and found a young, sympathetic lawyer willing to help us for very little money. He also agreed that we were in charge. We needed only a body with a local bar card: no time or effort, and certainly no interference.

Our local counsel played his role well. He sat with us and did nothing during our court appearances, so Judge Brett had the good sense and compassion to announce our local lawyer would no longer need to be in court. Glen and I knew our stuff, and the Judge knew we had extremely limited funds to pay another lawyer. I established our client's poverty status in declarations and motions to issue subpoenas and file papers in *pro per* – without the ordinary fees. This decision came as another relief.

U nfortunately, we lacked an impartial interpreter. Certified interpreters for Spanish speakers were supposedly not available in the Northern District of Oklahoma. The court searched for one in the civilian sector. The one the court found just happened to be the wife of a County District Attorney.

I objected. This interpreter had no training. Surely the greater Tulsa area held someone other than a prosecutor's wife! The judge ruled against us.

Judge Brett also refused to let Lucas help us talk to David and Emilio. Lucas was a defendant. David and Emilio were now witnesses subpoenaed by the prosecution. They were prepared to take the Fifth, refusing to testify on the grounds that what they said might be used against them.

Prosecutor Ben Baker demanded to talk to David and Emilio without their lawyers present. We objected. The prosecutor might try to talk our clients out of asserting their Fifth Amendment rights, using threats and intimidation. The judge finally ruled that Ben could talk to them. It was a short conversation. Our cleients had nothing to say to him.

Baker then argued that the Fifth Amendment couldn't be invoked because charges against David and Emilio had already been dismissed. We pointed out that other charges might still be brought. Judge Brett agreed and ruled the Fifth Amendment would apply unless the prosecutor granted them *use immunity*, meaning their testimony couldn't be used against them. Ben Baker refused.

The D.A.'s wife served as interpreter. She spoke formal Spanish, not colloquial Salvadoran or Mexican Spanish. Court interpreters required different skills and training other than being fluent in two languages. Her skills were not called into action. David and Emilio refused to testify.

Judge Brett had one amusing habit. His bailiff was required by law or custom to command, "All Rise!" as the judge entered the courtroom. A modest man, the judge walked in from a side door. His body language and the look on his face always said, "Oh my, please, please sit down. This is too much."

I had to stifle a laugh each time. I wondered why the judge didn't simply instruct his bailiff to stop telling everyone to rise!

Forced to defend themselves, Carol and Lucas wanted to put U.S. foreign policy on trial to expose complicity in the brutal repression in El Salvador. If our system had followed its own laws, David and Emilio would have refugee status, and it would have been no crime to ride in a car with them. But INS had to follow the U.S. official position, claiming that El Salvador was a democracy, not a repressive regime. Establishing refugee status seemed highly unlikely, probably futile.

We felt we could make a strong case for repression in El Salvador. We could also prove that no refugees from the civil wars in Central America were being granted political asylum, in spite of raging wars, widespread political oppression, dictatorships, and death squads.

Virtually everyone escaping Cuba received automatic political asylum. No showing of repression or fear for one's own safety was required. Similar status went to refugees from other countries the U.S. had labeled as "enemies."

This same issue would become central to the sanctuary trials a few years later. Several U.S. religious denominations joined in the sanctuary movement to challenge government policy by openly granting sanctuary to Central American refugees who arrived here without papers. Volunteers drove them to work, the store, the doctor – all technically illegal actions. In 1984, the government started prosecuting the most visible and active of these defiant sanctuary leaders – including Catholic nuns – primarily in Texas and Arizona.

But in 1984 the U.S. prosecutors in these high-profile sanctuary cases developed a strategy of filing pretrial motions to preclude trial testimony and any argument that the sanctuary leaders believed the immigrants were entitled to political refugee status. This put a higher burden of proof on the defendants in a pre-trial hearing with a judge, not a jury. Some of those sanctuary leaders were convicted and sent to prison. Even after being paroled, they would, for the rest of their lives, suffer the stigma and discrimination that followed ex-cons.

The Deputy U.S. Attorney assigned to our cases was Ben Baker, a veteran Tulsa prosecutor who wore a cowboy hat and boots. A conservative, he imparted a negative attitude toward Central American revolutionaries, communists, or what my legal partner in this effort, Glen Van Slyke, liked to call, "what-not." I don't know if Ben Baker detested our clients, us, our entourage, our cause, or all of the above – but he refused to talk directly to me or to Glen. This was the only time I experienced this treatment in my 25 years as a lawyer.

Ben Baker's refusal to talk to us caused strange logistic problems. Informal discussions between counsel are the usual way of resolving many trial issues, big and small. Francis "Frank" Keating was the head U.S. Attorney in the Northern District of Oklahoma at the time, and was reduced to acting as interpreter for Ben Baker. When meetings of counsel were necessary, they were held in Keating's big, corner office, using Keating as an interpreter. Instead of speaking directly to us, Baker spoke to Keating, then Keating repeated what Baker just said even though we heard it, then we responded to Keating, who relayed our message to Baker, even though Baker just heard us – and so on.

161

Everyone knew that Keating was a rising Republican star at the time. Maybe he was nice to everyone. Indeed, he become Governor of Oklahoma from 1995-2003, a front-runner for the GOP vice-presidential nomination in 2000, then on the short list for G.W. Bush's first Attorney General.

An unusual calm fell over us between Christmas and New Year. Everyone else was with family, friends, happily distracted. Glen and Mara spent time in Kentucky with family and at home in Houston. David, Emilio, and our helpers were out of town. Carol, Lucas, Betsy and I were stuck in Tulsa, with nothing but this case in our lives and no one but each other. We nervously awaited the final act of a drama begun at a toll booth in the pre-dawn hours almost three months ago. All our motions had been written, all the witnesses lined up. Trial was set for Monday, January 4th.

We treated ourselves to a movie, then Christmas dinner at Bordens, an old-fashioned cafeteria chain. When I signed the credit card slip, the cashier blurted out that my signature was "the most ridiculous thing I've ever seen!" Even during the holidays, criticism was served daily in Tulsa.

Dinner had been otherwise uneventful. Our conversation had been subdued. The whole scene felt surreal: the cafeteria and adjoining mall where we saw the movie stood virtually empty. We were sitting in the middle of the lull before a storm.

Warren Beatty starred as American journalist John Reed. Set during the Russian revolution. *Reds* came out to great fanfare a few weeks earlier. We were too busy to take time off then. The epic film ran nearly three and one-half hours. It presented a heroic picture of the downtrodden rising up against centuries of tsarist exploitation and oppression. It was, of course, criticized for presenting a sympathetic portrait of John Reed and the revolutionaries – and for being too long. For us, it was inspiring, and a welcome distraction.

I still had some research to do in the week between Christmas and New Year but the law library was closed. I knew the staff pretty well by then and talked a friendly librarian into driving over to the library and letting me in a few times that week. She trusted me and let me work alone and close up when I was through. It was very eerie being alone in a large law library for hours at a time, but seemed completely appropriate under the circumstances. Witnesses and helpers would start arriving in a few days. Toward the end of the week, we were driving back and forth to the airport bringing people on board for the trial. Monday morning we were as ready as we'd ever be.

The Trial

W
e were in trial from 9-to-5 during the first week of January, 1982. The prosecution subpoenaed David and Emilio to testify against Carol and Lucas. Presumably Ben Baker wanted to ask what Carol and Lucas knew about their immigration status. What Carol and Lucas knew was key to the case.

There were the usual last-minute logistic discussions that morning, and Ben tried to keep us away from David and Emilio so that his people could talk to and threaten them without interference. I wouldn't let them do that, so they complained to the judge who finally ordered me to let them have another short interview outside my presence. But David and Emilio were tough, politically astute, and solidly on board with the defense. Again they refused to talk to the prosecutor or to testify in court.

Border Patrol agents testified about the arrest and their questioning of the four, their reasons to believe that David and Emilio were in the U.S. illegally, and the communist literature in the car (now "evidence"), including articles about the repression, resistance and revolutions in Central America. There were fliers about Salvadoran revolutionaries on a speaking tour about El Salvador, but no evidence that Carol and Lucas knew David and Emilio were here illegally.

Most juries don't take it seriously, but the burden of proof rests on the prosecution, so it was important to show that the prosecution had no direct evidence of what Carol and Lucas knew or didn't know. Still, we felt the need to give the jury something else to consider. We intended to put the case in context of the U.S. policy of supporting overt dictatorships and death-squad regimes. We presented what evidence we could about political repression in El Salvador.

Our best witness turned out to be acclaimed poet Carolyn Forche. We heard about her through Central American activist networks. She taught English at the University of Arkansas, just across the border. As a writer and activist, she visited Central America during the early days of rebellions and death-squads, and wrote an award-winning book of poems, *The Country Between Us*. I couldn't believe my luck when I phoned her at the English Department and she agreed to testify and stay in Tulsa as long as needed.

Carolyn was incredibly generous with her time, spending most of the trial week with us in town. Fluent in Spanish, she got to know David and Emilio and the small entourage there to help us. Her court testimony described the atmosphere of repression in El Salvador, the death squads, the activists who had disappeared, and the murder of Archbishop Romero one day after his sermon that called on Salvadoran soldiers to obey God's higher order and to stop carrying out governmental violations of human rights. Judge Brett let the poet have her say, and it was powerful.

On Friday afternoon, the jury came back deadlocked. The judge dismissed them. We were not permitted talk to the jury after the trial, but we believed they had hung on the issue of whether Carol and Lucas had a good-faith belief that David and Emilio were political refugees. Happy to be alive to fight another day, we remained disappointed. Another trial, with more pre-trial motions, seemed probable.

Dear Kathy,
Send more clothes!

Tired and cold as we descended the courthouse steps that afternoon of Friday, January 8th, we were ready to relax and celebrate. Instead, we were forced to evacuate our home immediately and find other places for everyone to stay.

A front-page headline in the evening *Tulsa World* blared COMMUNISTS IN TULSA. The article listed the address of our home/office/headquarters on Page One. It repeated our address on an inside page. For us, this represented an open invitation to every drunk or jingoistic hothead with a gun rack in a pick-up truck to drive by and pop off a few rounds in our direction – or worse. We wondered if Ben Baker knew any of the staff at the *Tulsa World* and if he was having a good laugh.

We quickly loaded cars with our belongings, then stood at pay phones on a freezing cold evening trying to find places to stay. Only a few of us knew anyone in Tulsa. We didn't have enough money for separate motel rooms, but pooling our funds, we rented one room. There, we could stay warm, shower, make phone calls, and arrange getting out of town.

Those who had arrived by car left right away. We took the others to airports over the next few days. We found friends who might put a few of us up for a while. One thing remained certain: we couldn't go back to the house on Latimer Street.

The Aftermath

Then there were two.

Carol stayed with local anti-war poet, Mary McAnally. I stayed with a local law professor whom I had known as a student at UC-Santa Barbara.

Monday morning found me back at the law library, researching and preparing post-trial motions, including a motion to dismiss the case on the ground that a second jury couldn't reasonably convict Carol and Lucas on the evidence presented at the first trial.

I spent several days in the library, filed the motions in mid-January, then waited for Ben Baker to respond and the judge to render a decision.

My law professor friend, Chuck, lived alone in a large, two-story home near the Arkansas River. A runner in those days, I would lope along the river path. By the end of January, I felt in good enough shape to handle the Tulsa half-marathon. During those weeks, I was able to relax and reflect on the madness I'd been through since Carol's phone call back in October.

I researched another problem while I waited. David and Emilio faced deportation proceedings, and their cases would be heard in the Dallas office of the Immigration and Naturalization Service. We desperately needed the case to be transferred to L.A., where both of them lived and where we had support and resources. We expected a battle over political asylum in those deportation proceedings. With no contacts in Dallas, we would be at a terrible disadvantage, and David and Emilio would suffer because of that.

The provision for formally requesting the District Director (DD) of INS to transfer a case to another district allowed great discretion in granting or denying a request. The DD wasn't even required to make a ruling! I discovered that DDs rarely made any ruling. They usually let the case proceed wherever it had been assigned.

My research turned up an interesting tidbit. If the DD formally denied our request, we could file suit in District Court to challenge that denial. Even better, we could file the suit in Los Angeles – the official residence of our clients, my home, and the warm, sunny venue of our dreams. However, if the DD made no ruling, there could be no change of venue, no appeal, no recourse for us.

Our challenge then, would be to get the DD to take some action. In late January, Carol and I flew to Dallas. At a press conference, we announced our intention to file a motion for change of venue. We issued a press release and made statements accusing INS of being part of a conspiracy to silence dissent and to condemn Central Americans like David and Emilio to torture and death. If any sense of justice prevailed in the system, INS would give our clients a fair chance in L.A.

My brazen statements were intended to provoke the DD to act. It worked! In a press release denying our "outrageous allegations," the Dallas DD announced his formal denial of our motion.

I'd like to think I outwitted him – that he unknowingly took my bait and handed us a valuable gift on a silver platter. But maybe he just wanted to get rid of us.

On February 7, Judge Brett granted our motion to dismiss the case against Carol and Lucas on the ground that a second jury could not reasonably find them guilty in another trial. The next day, I was at the Tulsa airport again, this time dropping-off the rental car and going home for the first time in four months. The last of all of us to leave, I felt as though I was pulling some kind of ladder up behind me.

Being back home and seeing Kathy and my son was wonderful, of course, but I knew that The Salvador Tour Case wasn't over. A few weeks later, I filed suit in District Court against the Dallas DD, challenging his denial of a change of venue. Faced with the prospect of defending a civil suit in Los Angeles, the DD transferred the cases to L.A., and our suit was dropped.

Living at home and working at a more leisurely pace, I would litigate the political asylum cases for David and Emilio over the next four years. During that time, the public became more aware of what was really going on in Central America and there was much more evidence to prove our case.

Feature from the L.A. Downtown News.

And there was more willingness to accept our evidence and to take it seriously. In 1986 we had a long hearing and presented volumes of evidence of political repression in El Salvador to a fair judge who eventually split the baby in half, denying political asylum, a permanent status, but granting "withholding of deportation," which was almost as good.

As a practical matter, David and Emilio were allowed to stay in the United States until political conditions in El Salvador changed for the better, which seemed a long way off.

VI

L.A. REVISITED

In the Halls of Justice,
the only justice is in the halls.
— National Lawyers Guild

A Mosh Pit of Justice

W hen I returned from Tulsa in February, 1982, several of my lawyer friends had started using personal computers and Xerox machines in their small practices. Large companies and offices had been using this technology for a while. The military was first to adopt it. Typewriters and carbon paper were becoming part of the past. I had been gone only four months, banging away on a non-electric public typewriter at the University of Tulsa Law Library. Culture and technology had somehow jumped way ahead without me.

A public defender, assigned to misdemeanor cases, Kathy knew lots of people in the criminal courts building by this time. Our victory in Tulsa made big news among friends, allies and those following the case closely – and Kathy was proud of us. She introduced me to arraignment and preliminary hearing judges who appointed lawyers to cases of defendants that a public defender couldn't take, usually because of a potential conflict with a witness or another defendant. Private attorneys would then be appointed and paid a modest fee by the county, as I had previously experienced in many of the political cases.

I took these cases to pay the bills. I rented space in a very low-rent building down a flight of stairs from Sunset Boulevard in Echo Park. It served as a place to work – more like a basement than a typical a law office. I would meet my clients in these misdemeanor cases either in court or in coffee shops. I hired Michael Hughes, a bright and enthusiastic recent graduate of Southwestern law school, who helped me with the cases and took on a few of his own. We became lifelong friends and worked together until he got his "dream job" with the California Attorney General.

A small sweatshop stood across the hall from our office. Nicaraguan women worked at sewing machines all day. In spite of the lint and fibers littering the halls and stairs, that office served me well for two years. Between our house and the office and the courts, I could take one of four bus lines that traveled along that stretch of Sunset Boulevard.

172

Even on a terrible day, working close to home was a positive.

One of my more interesting court-appointed cases began normally enough, but evolved into several other, larger cases.

I went into lock-up behind an arraignment court one morning to meet Sammy, the client I was appointed to represent. He and another man, Ron, were charged with misdemeanor assault on deputy sheriffs in the jail across the street. Sammy seemed comfortable when Ron joined our confidential discussion. We covered procedures and scheduling, leaving the details of the case to be dealt with after the arraignment.

I expected to be entering a plea of not guilty and to delay the case a few weeks. Judges provided a lot of flexibility in scheduling as long as the defendant would waive time, legal-speak for giving up the right to a speedy trial within 10 days. Defendants rarely objected.

Sammy and Ron, however, knew the system. Both had been in jail – Ron on a murder charge, Sammy for armed robbery – at the time of their fracas with two deputies in the notorious Hall of Justice jail (HOJJ). That facility housed mostly hard-core defendants awaiting trial and prison. It was the same place I had seen Charles Manson and talked with Geronimo Pratt back in 1971.

This little misdemeanor case paled in comparison to the felony charges against Sammy and Ron. But they were pissed off at the deputies, and they wanted to win. Each had been through the criminal justice system and thought they'd have a better chance if the trial started before the D.A. and the witnesses could get their stories straight. They refused to waive time. I realized they would not budge. I also realized that they had a good point.

The case was set for trial within 10 days. It was common to trail – wait, in court lingo– up to 10 more days for an empty courtroom. My co-counsel, Randy Sortino, was friendly and low-key, someone I could get along with. We informed the court that our clients would not waive time. I explained that we would present pre-trial motions. That got us assigned to Judge Pattie Jo McKay, a patient and thoughtful judge. For some reason, she never could get Randy's last name right. She added an extra syllable, calling him "Mr. Sorentino."

Randy's client, Ron, stood 6'4" and weighed 250 pounds. The deputies believed him to be a hit man for a Blood gang. Considered very dangerous, he was housed in HOJJ accordingly. One large, white, weight-lifting deputy apparently felt challenged by Ron and took every opportunity to give him trouble. One morning, Ron and the deputy started fighting. Sammy happened to be in the same area. Another deputy came in and, thinking Sammy was part of the fight, attacked him.

The four men went at it until other deputies unlocked the door and joined the fray. Nobody was seriously injured, but deputies claimed that other inmates hit and grabbed them, and threw cups of urine on them through the bars during the brawl.

We made an unusual request to allow the jury to see the scene of the crime. The jail stood across Temple Street on the 11th floor of the old Hall of Justice, now the Sheriff's department headquarters. After consulting with colleagues and the sheriff, the judge okayed our field trip.

Randy and I prepared for trial, reviewing reports, talking to our clients and other inmate witnesses. This case felt more interesting than most, and the judge seemed to like it. She gave us some leeway to ask questions and prove our case: Ron had been the victim, simply defending himself and not the aggressor; Sammy had been an observer, forced to defend himself from an attack by the second deputy.

Tunnels led between the criminal courthouse and the Hall of Justice, which served as the main courthouse in L.A. for decades. When L.A. outgrew the facility, the county built a criminal courts building on the next block, continuing to use the top three floors of the Hall of Justice as a convenient jail for those awaiting trial across the street. Over the years, it became a jail for the hard-core.

So one morning, the judge and her staff, the lawyers, the jury, and the defendants, followed a security detail of deputies to service elevators that opened to the tunnel

174

under the street. More service elevators took us all into the Hall of Justice and up to a remote section of that dark old jail.

This quick tour would put the testimony in perspective for everyone. Though I had been to that jail many times, I had never been in the area where the fight took place. The halls and cells seemed smaller than I remembered. What we were seeing didn't fit the picture the deputies painted on the witness stand. For one thing, all the action described in the testimony occurred inside a small, dingy area with iron bars everywhere. *Duck your head!*

The jury would find Ron and Sammy not guilty. Even the judge seemed pleased by the verdict. Randy and I worked together as a team. That had been my standard approach in the political cases. Like political defendants, Sammy and Ron enjoyed a common theme and had no conflict of interest. Sammy was so impressed, he asked me to represent him in the armed robbery case against him. Unfortunately, we weren't so lucky that time. The evidence offered me little to work with. Sammy went to prison again.

Meanwhile, I talked to my friend Robert Mann about filing a civil rights suit in federal court for the beating Sammy and Ron experienced. Several other men had been roughed up and handcuffed in that incident. Ron and Sammy had no problem getting six other inmates to join our effort. We filed a civil rights suit in federal court.

During this time, Ron asked me to stand in for him in his murder case, only to request a continuance. He claimed to be raising money to hire Johnny Cochran, one of L.A.'s best and most famous criminal defense lawyers. Legally, standing in is not holding someone's place in line, so I knew I would become Ron's attorney of record until Cochran could show up at the next court appearance. The judge would give me a courtesy continuance because I was new on the case, but that would be as good as it got.

Ron agreed that I would not be representing him at trial. I believed him. He had been straight with me and impressed me as a serious guy with connections. I thought he was someone who could hire Johnny Cochran.

The other reason I trusted Ron stemmed from my own lack of familiarity with his case. I thought he would not be stupid enough to go to court in a murder case with a lawyer unprepared for trial. I was wrong.

R on's case was set in the courtroom of Judge Clarence "Red" Stromwall, a well-known former member of the LAPD Hat Squad, later immortalized in the 1996 film *Mulholland Falls*. The Hat Squad worked out of the robbery division after WWII into the early 60's. It reported only to the Chief of Police, who authorized broad license to squad members to drive gangsters out of Los Angeles.

In 1987, following the death of squad leader Max Herman (played by Nick Nolte in the movie) LAPD spokesman Lt. Dan Cook noted:

> "The clothing was part of their mystique. They were impeccably dressed, impressive physical specimens of men who established a national reputation for tough-ness. They were so feared and respected that when we'd announce that such and such a case had been turned over to the Hat Squad, many of the suspects in those cases would voluntarily give themselves up."

The reputation of The Hats applied to Red Stromwall, a ruddy-faced judge who always looked as if he'd been drinking with the boys after lunch – maybe even before lunch. He granted Ron a continuance, but made clear he didn't like it. Suspicious of defendants and defense lawyers playing games, Judge Stromwall told me that if Johnny Cochran wasn't in court on the day of trial, I would have to start without him.

I waited anxiously. Cochran didn't call to say he'd be there. In court early, I waited in the hall, hoping to see him walk around the corner from the elevators. If he showed up he would have no trouble getting another continuance. Johnny never showed up.

As promised, Judge Stromwall held no sympathy for my desperate argument that I was completely unprepared and couldn't possibly represent Ron adequately. As a last ditch plea– and in order to assist an appeal – I said, "You can't convict a man whose lawyer is completely unprepared!"

Red Stromwall answered: "Bring in the jury panel."

LOS ANGELES POLICE DEPARTMENT

DARYL F. GATES
Chief of Police

TOM BRADLEY
Mayor

P. O. Box 30158
Los Angeles, Calif. 90030
Telephone:
(213)- 485-3291
Refd: 4.1

June 18, 1985

Mr. Richard Elden
1252 West First Street
Los Angeles, California 90026

Dear Mr. Elden:

Your June 4, 1985 correspondence to Chief Daryl F. Gates has been referred to this office for investigation and response.

Your characterization of police conduct on April 24 in Pershing Square is without foundation in fact or law. Not necessarily related to "No Business As Usual", fifteen juvenile truants were detained in the vicinity of Pershing Square and were then released to their parents. You rely on the case of In Re James (1984) 164 CAL. APP 3d 515. The City Attorney's review of the official reports discloses that the California Supreme Court granted a hearing in that case on March 21, 1985, and as a result, the decision of the Court of Appeals has been vacated.

Your second complaint is being formally investigated via the personnel complaint process. You will be informed of the results of that investigation at its conclusion.

It is not the policy of the Los Angeles Police Department to prevent people from participating in lawful political protests. It is the Department's intention to provide the best possible police service while maintaining the rights of individuals.

Very truly yours,

DARYL F. GATES
Chief of Police

B. R. WEDGEWORTH, Captain
Commanding Officer
Central Area

AN EQUAL EMPLOYMENT OPPORTUNITY—AFFIRMATIVE ACTION EMPLOYER

Letter from the LAPD.

I worked with a talented private investigator in those days. Sue Sarkis was a two-fisted, gun-toting New York transplant who also served as my bail bondswoman. I asked her to find the witnesses named in the two-page police report. That was all I had to go on.

Ron was alleged to have shot a guy in the front seat of a Ford Bronco parked in darkness on a residential street. Two different neighbors told the police they had heard the gunshots and had seen a man run from the car. Each described that man as standing 5'8" to 5'10" and weighing 150 to 170 pounds. That man could not be Ron.

The only physical evidence against Ron was his fingerprint on a paper bag inside the Bronco. That proved he had touched the paper bag at some point, nothing more. If Sue could find one of those two neighbors, we could put them on the witness stand and win this damn thing.

She searched for them on the first day while I took my time picking the jury. On the second day she got a current address for one of the witnesses. He wasn't home when she went by that morning. She had other things to do, so I drove to his house during our lunch break. Luckily, I found him there and served him with a subpoena. Showing him the police report, I talked to him about his testimony, then took him to court with me. I called him to the stand that afternoon.

Asked to describe the man he saw running from the Bronco after the gunshots, the witness testified to the same information he gave in the police report. And I earned an easy *not guilty* verdict in my first and only murder trial.

In my opinion, the D.A. acted irresponsibly and unethically in prosecuting someone he must have known to be innocent. Corroborating statements by the two eye witnesses alone should have convinced him someone else committed this crime. Except for a fingerprint on a paper bag in the vehicle, no evidence linked Ron to the victim, the location, the Bronco, or the murder. Perhaps the D.A. saw Ron only as a gang member and an alleged hit man. Maybe that was enough to charge him. The actual killer was never apprehended or prosecuted. Unfortunately, I saw this happen too often.

All in all, I handled three criminal trials for Ron and Sammy and came out on top twice. Not bad for a criminal defense lawyer. Our won-lost percentage tends to be much lower, mainly because the police and prosecutors usually hold all the high cards of evidence.

Now only one civil case remained. I had done a lot of the work, but I would be depending on Robert Mann to lead in the pre-trial and trial proceedings. He was more familiar with federal civil practices and procedures, and had tried more civil cases before juries.

On the morning of trial, the other seven plaintiffs were still in custody. Only Ron was released. Some smart lawyer got him off on a murder case. Of course, that same lawyer was not smart enough to get paid!

Dressed in black suits and ties, Ron and two other large men looked more like members of the Nation of Islam than Bloods. After last-minute negotiations, the county presented a reasonable settlement offer. We discussed the offer with the seven other defendants as a group in lockup, and hammered out an acceptable division of the money.

Ron and his bodyguards rejected the split that all the others had agreed on. He felt he deserved more money. He had a point. He suffered the most abuse in the fight, received the most injuries, and was one of only two who were prosecuted.

We had already allocated the highest sum to him, a little less to Sammy, and far less to the six who weren't injured or prosecuted. Part of Ron's unhappiness came from owing me money. He hadn't paid me for his murder case, so I would now be taking that fee out of his share, leaving him with less that he expected. Robert and I knew that this deal was the best we could get, fair to everyone. Rejecting it, we could get nothing. But Ron wouldn't agree, and we couldn't accept the deal without him. I worried that he thought I couldn't lose after what I'd done for him so far.

Finally, I asked him to walk down the hall with me, away from his bodyguards. I looked up into the face of this alleged hit man towering above me, and told him I wasn't about to let him screw up a hard-won deal for everyone else. We all wanted to settle this case, get some money, and stop getting up at 3 a.m. to wait in line to get on a bus and go to court, only to wait again – something Ron knew only too well to be a huge pain in the ass.

I have no idea why he changed his mind – certainly I couldn't intimidate him – but he finally agreed to the proposal. Everybody lived happily ever after.

Not really.

Civil Rights
and Police Misconduct Cases

I met Henry Giler in the '70s. An older man, he had served in the Abraham Lincoln Brigade – American volunteers in the Spanish Civil War against fascist Generalissimo Francisco Franco, an ally of Hitler. As a leftist, Henry was active in the union movement before and after fighting in Spain.

With a special interest in government repression and police issues, he believed lawyers should fight police misconduct–maybe even make some money by taking more cases and winning them. The cost of litigation, settlements, and verdicts would eventually come to the attention of the City Council or the Board of Supervisors. That might persuade them do something to rein in police abuse. Since I had worked for the ACLU's police misconduct complaint centers in law school, Henry asked me to attend a series of meetings that would help found the Police Misconduct Lawyer Referral Service (PMLRS) in 1979, later known as Police Watch.

Defending criminal cases in the '80s, I grew frustrated with the tendency of juries to disbelieve the testimony of defendants and to believe any crazy-ass thing the police might say from the witness stand. "It looked like a gun" became the blanket justification for a police shooting. Juries might look at my client's testimony differently in a civil case, where my client became the plaintiff, not the defendant. I began handling police misconduct cases and became more active in PMLRS and its monthly educational meetings, run by NLG lawyer Hugh Manes.

In 1988, I joined a group of PMLRS lawyers in representing several plaintiffs in a major case against the LAPD. Most of us had known each other for years, but we never handled a case together as a team. It sounded promising.

In a pre-dawn raid on two apartments on Dalton Ave., 88 officers entered looking for drugs. At least one of these officers went berserk, destroying tables, beds, chests of drawers, coffee tables, TVs, kitchen and bathroom sinks, counters, toilets, cupboards – almost everything.

Holes were punched in every wall of every room. Broken door frames dangled from their jambs. The rear stairs now hung precariously over the back yard, unusable. The destruction was stunning, and undeniably inexcusable. Only a small amount of drugs was found in one of the two apartments. There was nothing to justify such a large-scale raid and so much destruction.

The evidence indicated that the destruction of the two apartments happened in spite of extensive preparations for serving a warrant. There had even been a rehearsal a few days earlier, with a command post and senior officers on the scene. Dozens of officers saw this one berserk cop engage in wanton destruction over a long period of time. Apparently, none of them did anything to stop him.

The case produced outrage. It disgraced the LAPD and the city. We took it very seriously, and the city knew it had a lot at stake. Our team of experienced lawyers presented a formidable threat that would expose the truth. A huge verdict could be predicted. I made that clear at the very first deposition.

I walked in with the lead plaintiff: a black, middle-aged housewife and mother. Prosecutors and LAPD liaisons were chatting it up, laughing and joking as if at a Friday happy hour. Their attitude turned me off. I glared at them, refusing to greet or smile at any of them, even those I knew. I can remember thinking, *I'm glad you're having a good time. Now let's get on with kicking your ass!* Message received.

Early on, police department attorneys offered to settle the case for $3.5 million. That included a nice payday for the lawyers, because we hadn't yet done much work. Faced with devastating evidence, the city didn't want this case to get any attention. It worked out well for our clients, too. They didn't own the damaged apartments and they had suffered no physical injuries.

Lynwood Sheriff and Batts Case

With the Dalton Ave. case, we began regular case meetings. We continued that practice for years, moving from one case to another. Our second big case proved more difficult, took much more time, and lasted years.

Black and Latino clients told stories of unjust and illegal activity by the Lynwood station of the Sheriff's Department: illegal searches of homes, cars and people, false arrest, brutality, murder. Reports revealed that the Lynwood station had its own gang of Deputies who went beyond the law to punish those they considered gangsters – a modern version of the Hat Squad.

During these years of the war on drugs, police focused on black neighborhoods across the country, looking for drugs and receiving federal money for drug arrests. The media cooperated with government and politicians in promoting widespread fear of black gangs – especially Bloods and Crips – and "super predators" in neighborhoods labeled as super-dangerous "jungles." The resulting hysteria made it easy for police to overreact, commit crimes themselves, and get away with them. The harshest critics claimed the police were getting away with murder.

My main job concentrated on defending a criminal case for an Original Gangster (O.G.) or elder of a Crips gang well known in Lynwood. Tracy Batts, the O.G., and his brother Tim had been charged with firing 15 AK-47 rounds from a moving car at two deputies driving in a patrol car. The deputies were not hit, but the patrol car was allegedly disabled by eight rounds.

Tim was arrested shortly after the incident. Tracy stayed on the run for a year before getting arrested. During that year, Tim went to trial and was found not guilty. The prosecutor had no evidence of who did the shooting, only the eyewitness identification by the deputies. Jurors found reasonable doubt of the deputies' ability to identify Tim under the difficult circumstances of two moving cars at night, multiple gunshots, and whatever else might have been happening on Rosecrans Avenue that night.

183

Arrested after Tim's acquittal, Tracy gave me permission to use the criminal case for discovery, a process that might be useful in both the criminal and civil cases. This required him to "waive time" and let us continue the case.

Procedure manuals and our experience told us that a crime like this one should have generated a slew of individual and supervisor reports, radio calls, log entries, photographs, lab reports, as well as physical evidence. I made motions and got solid, specific and comprehensive discovery orders. The prosecutor gave me less than I anticipated – a lot less, just the standard amount any typical criminal case might yield. Analyzing the evidence, I made motions for specific things I had not been given. I subpoenaed staff in the Sheriff's Department to prove more evidence existed and that we were entitled to see it. Another discovery order, another hearing.

My partner, Dan Callaway, and I believed Tracy and Tim were framed because of their gang affiliation. We needed evidence from the Sheriff's own files to prove it. Even then, no smoking gun would likely be found. We would have to rely on circumstantial evidence.

We dragged our feet and refused to go to trial until we had every report, log, scrap of paper, disabled-car-repair invoice, and every radio call that could shed light on what actually happened that night. If we could prove that Tim and Tracy were deliberately being framed for something they didn't do, Tracy would walk free. And our civil case against the Sheriff's Department would be greatly enhanced.

Every time we appeared in court, the prosecutor would announce he was ready for trial, and then argued strenuously against any further continuance. The judge probably agreed. He may have wanted to get this trial over with, but he couldn't ignore the facts or our legal arguments. And we could always show that the D.A. and Sheriff's Department were still withholding evidence.

On that basis, we kept telling the judge that it wasn't our fault we were not prepared for trial. Time after time, I risked my reputation ("I'm not prepared.") and the judge's anger ("I will not proceed with this trial.").

Tracy knew he was being framed for a serious crime, with serious prison time on the line. He was willing to sit in jail and waive time whenever we demanded a continuance. He backed our legal play. That meant a lot to us.

Our dogged approach and Tracy's patience would soon pay off.

☮

We discovered evidence that undermined the official version of a cop car being shot while in service. We demonstrated that other evidence was missing or destroyed. And it got better.

I questioned one deputy in a pre-trial hearing who admitted that a semi-secret, invitation-only group of "hard chargers" calling themselves Vikings existed within the Sheriff's Department. Members sported a Viking tattoo on their ankles. In a dramatic courtroom moment, the judge granted my request for the deputy to lift his pant leg. I carefully described his tattoo, including the Viking helmet and the words *Chongo Fighter*, for the record.

A knock-down, drag-out legal battle lasted longer than a year. Motions, subpoenas, court hearings, interviews, investigations, and going to the brink of both trial and contempt of court filled those months. We came to believe that the AK-47 attack described in the police reports never actually took place. Instead, that patrol car was damaged when deputies were horsing around that night. They shot up their own car to make it look like a drive-by. Then they tried to pin it on someone else – bad guys they wanted out of the way. Enter the two brothers, Tim and Tracy.

During that year, I repeatedly accused the Sheriff's Department and the District Attorney of framing Tim and Tracy, of hiding and destroying evidence, of lying to the court. My accusations were repeated in some local news outlets, including the *Long Beach Press Telegram*, picked up my accusations. Stories about the Lynwood deputies and their vigilante gang had already made news.

This combative atmosphere made it all the more surprising when, just prior to the trial starting for a third time, the D.A. suddenly offered us a sweet deal.

185

Tracy was charged with two counts of attempted murder of police officers with an AK-47, hitting the police car eight times. The D.A. would now lower the charge to simple felony assault. Tracy would get out of jail in two weeks with a "time served" sentence. We couldn't refuse this offer. He had resided in county jail for nearly two years – those years before I had taken on the case – and was facing two potential life sentences. Getting out in two weeks felt like a victory to him. To us, it felt like vindication of our claims that the brothers had been framed.

The surprise offer represented as a virtual concession that the case against Tracy was bogus from day one. And now, it was over.

Watching the L.A. Riots

The clerk in our case against the Lynwood Sheriff didn't like us, and seldom did us any favors. As far as she was concerned, we were nothing but name-callers and troublemakers. But she might have hated the work we created for her more than anything. We filed motions, demanded hearings, issued subpoenas, and took up a lot of the court's time and energy.

The clerk also didn't like that we had a tendency to upset the court's schedule. We filed papers at the last minute. She and the judge would tell us we couldn't do a certain thing and we would do it anyway. The first two times the trial was scheduled, we simply refused to start. We got away with it. The clerk hated us.

One of our court hearings was scheduled for a Thursday in April, 1992. On Tuesday, a jury in Simi Valley acquitted the LAPD officers who had beaten Rodney King with batons – 55 times, captured on video. Wednesday afternoon TV news aired what looked like the beginning of a riot in L.A.: the beating of truck driver Reginald Denny, attacks on LAPD's Parker Center, the Federal Courthouse, and other civic buildings downtown.

Watching this unfold on TV all afternoon and thinking things would probably get worse as night fell, I called court before the clerk went home. Dan Callaway and I would be leaving early from our office in Oceanside, at least 90 minutes away, and we wanted to know if "the court" would still be in session the next morning, given what was happening downtown. The clerk probably thought I was just trying to get out of a court appearance and to delay the case again. Curt and dismissive, she gave the impression that a little rioting couldn't possibly influence the mighty, white marble courthouse towering over the black residents of Compton and Lynwood. She made it clear that I'd better be there the next morning or I'd be in big trouble.

Images of the rebellion dominated local television all evening and through the night. Knowing L.A. as I did, I saw the action move west from downtown to the Korean district of N. Western Ave, then toward South Central, Watts and Compton. I was sure there would be little chance of our case being heard in the morning, but fearing the wrath and power of people aligned against us, Dan and I suited up that Thursday morning and met early at the office. We couldn't call the court because we had to leave Oceanside long before the clerk would get in.

We stopped at our usual breakfast place on North Long Beach Blvd, just south of the now-larger riot zone. After breakfast I used a pay phone to call the court and see if anyone would be there, if the courts would open, and if our case would still be heard. The news reported an attack on the Compton Courthouse the night before, but with no significant damage.

The clerk answered the phone and quickly confirmed that the courthouse was closed. Our case would be rescheduled when things returned to normal. I resisted the temptation to tell her, "I told you so."

Dan and I decided that since we were near L.A. and had set aside the day anyway, we'd drive around town and see what we could of the rioting.

We drove north to where the riot started the night before. Downtown was my old stomping grounds. Dan worked and went to law school nearby. It was amazing to see firsthand the reality of what we'd watched on TV the night before. The power and might of our institutions were brought low by an angry mob starved for justice.

Broken glass doors and windows were boarded up in front of Parker Center. The familiar entrance doors at the federal courthouse were broken, charred by fire, now covered with plywood. Yellow tape and cones marked areas and lanes where we couldn't drive. Glass still littered the street.

On North Western Ave., we saw the Korean stores and strip malls – all burned. We drove south on Western, past buildings in various stages of destruction by fire, from burned-out skeletons and smoldering embers to structures fully engulfed in flames. Firefighters shot water on some buildings. Some structures continued to burn unattended.

188

Stores were being looted. At more than one liquor store, we watched people working in ad hoc teams, prying the iron bars away from windows as others squeezed inside to hand bottles out to waiting hands. Close by, people carried large TV boxes to cars parked every which-way in an intersection. Some of those cars drove off with their trunks open, a huge cardboard box sticking out.

Several times we approached intersections that appeared to be blocked and impassable. Images of Reginald Denny being dragged out of his truck and beaten the night before were fresh on our minds. We didn't want to get stuck anywhere, unable to move. Whenever we doubted our ability to get through an upcoming intersection, we would turn onto the nearest side street, drive a few residential blocks and avoid potential danger.

Still, we had some close calls during the six hours we spent in the middle of a riot in progress. By mid-afternoon we made our way to Compton. All entrances to the mighty courthouse now wore yellow police tape. Squads of Deputies in riot gear stood guard, some holding leashes of police dogs. By then, we had seen enough. Tired, we headed back south for home.

VII

THE
STRUGGLE
CONTINUES

You can't say that civilization don't advance. . . for in every war they kill you a new way.

— WILL ROGERS

North County

In 1988, our son Joncannon was born and we decided to move from L.A. to North San Diego County to get away from our hectic lives and the big city. I continued to handle some L.A. cases from our new location. Since I didn't have a full-time job, I took more responsibility for the baby boy and the house.

In 1991, our daughter Katrina joined the family. With me working part time now, I put the kids in day care as needed. We found a wonderful, loving woman named Rosa, but finally decided that one of us should take care of our kids full-time. Kathy had a good job with benefits, and she liked being a public defender and a law teacher. I was unanimously picked to be a stay-at-home dad.

I was somewhat burned out and ready for a break from the feast-or-famine treadmill of practicing law, and disillusioned, too. The legal system reflects the bigger flaws in our society, and, with so much at stake, I felt frustration and disappointment contending against a wildly imperfect system and the tide of tradition and history. I put down my law books, thinking I might dust them off once both kids were enrolled in school.

When not taking care of the kids and the house, I checked out peace groups in San Diego and the local Amnesty International chapter (#471). I met some wonderful people, but didn't get involved beyond going to meetings and attending protests.

Most of the action took place in downtown San Diego. I lived 40 miles north, with small kids. I didn't know many liberals or progressives in North County. I held the popular view that there weren't many. I was wrong.

The Culture War in Vista
1992 - 1994

On the first Tuesday in November, 1992, the radical Christian right won a 3-2 majority on the Vista Unified School District Board of Trustees. After the election, a letter to the editor appeared in the local newspaper from the president of Americans United for Separation of Church and State, based in Silver Spring, Maryland. The letter cited a meeting that would be held locally at the Palomar Unitarian Universalist Fellowship, where a group would be formed to keep public schools secular. This major political issue sat squarely within my wheelhouse, and with two children coming up, I was especially interested.

In the '80s, the Moral Majority and other far-right Christian groups tried to make changes in public education at the state level. They succeeded in convincing several state legislatures to pass laws mandating the teaching of religious beliefs. Most of these laws were struck down by the courts.

After years of political and legal struggles, the Christian right changed strategies, shifting focus from state legislatures to local school districts. All over the country, their candidates ran for school boards disguised as the parents who were working to wrest God-given control of their children from an immoral, heartless, secular bureaucracy.

Teachers were portrayed as special interests. Moderate school boards were characterized as pawns of Godless teacher unions. Stealth candidates hid their true intentions and their ties to Christian-right organizations, like the Moral Majority and Focus on the Family.

The meeting turned out to be another turning point in my life. Not only did I meet like-minded people and become involved in local issues, I started attending the Fellowship with my daughter Katrina. As it was in Los Angeles, the local Unitarian Universalist Fellowship became a great place to find thoughtful people discussing important topics and taking action for social justice.

At the December Vista School Board meeting, the incoming board was asked about the rumors that it was going to eliminate evolution from the science curriculum. Board members said they would take it up at their next meeting. Word spread. Players on both sides began to organize.

The meeting room at the Vista School District headquarters could hold 60 to 80 people. Only half that number regularly attended the open meetings. A large turn-out was expected in January. The board moved the meeting to a school auditorium, with a capacity of 400.

More than 800 showed up. Those left outside banged on the windows and refused to let the meeting start until loudspeakers were set up so they could hear the proceedings.

National news networks sent reporters and cameras. Their satellite-equipped vans were parked outside, huge antennas aimed at the night sky. Inside, reporters, camera operators and photographers worked in cramped surroundings.

The tension felt palpable. Careful to conceal their own intentions, Board members listened as the speakers addressed evolution and science education. Passionate voices came from both sides, including heads of churches and other concerned organizations.

In one of the most dramatic moments, a San Diego State University professor lugged a heavy leather briefcase to the podium. He pulled out what looked like a large, pointed rock. It was actually the horn of a dinosaur, some 68 million years old. He asked how anyone could tell science teachers how to teach without believing that dinosaurs lived on Earth long before humans first appeared?

The Board took no action at that meeting. It decided to lay low on science for a while. Instead, the new conservative majority's first battle tackled Sex Education. The aim: replace a comprehensive Sex-Ed program with one touted by the Christian right. We mobilized parent and community opposition. Teachers organized their own opposition to the board, but coordinated with us.

For most of the first six months of 1993, the Board neglected other important issues. Sex-Ed was taught exclusively in the 7th grade. This new, arbitrary controversy focused on one class, at one grade level. It looked like something straight out of the radical right playbook. Big on symbolism, these Christian conservative Board members were pushing religious policies destined to be struck down by the courts as unconstitutional.

In opposition to the religious agenda, parents, teachers and community members in the district formed CAPE (Community Action for Public Education). We attended Vista School Board meetings in force, handed out informational leaflets, spoke at the podium. We wrote letters to the editor, op-ed pieces, appeared as guests on local radio. Our struggle caught the attention of the broader media.

One day, this stay-at-home dad conducted an interview with ABC News in the driveway of our home. The interview would be featured that night on the national news. Katrina, age 3 and riding her tricycle in the background, made her national television debut!

Maybe it was best that the Vista School Board didn't have time for other issues. Left alone, the schools were doing fine. When the Board finally turned to evolution and science, it tried to weaken the district science guidelines. One part of the new majority's strategy called for introducing a new textbook: *Of Pandas and People*. The concept of "Intelligent Design" would become an alternative to evolution. As a theory, Intelligent Design looked at the complexity of the natural world and concluded it could not have occurred by chance – there must have been a designer. God, of course, must be that designer. This text book, however, carefully avoided naming the designer, attempting to hide the true religious agenda.

In the second year of our opposition to the conservative majority, we relabeled ourselves the Coalition for Mainstream Education and worked to recall two Board trustees. (The third radical Christian trustee was up for reelection anyway.)

The first phase proved the hardest. We needed 10,000 valid signatures of district voters on our petition. We had support within the community. Many voters got friends to sign the petition, but didn't have the time or inclination to take the petition to the general public. Tempted to use paid signature gatherers, we determined to do it with volunteers.

I enjoy talking with strangers about important issues, so I jumped into the job of gathering signatures. We set up a table outside each Vista School Board meeting. We had someone with a clipboard and petitions outside the local Farmer's Market (they wouldn't let us in). But we could go to grocery stores any time, and they were our most productive locations. We wrote letters to the editor and took advantage of every possible opportunity to get signatures and to promote our cause.

My children often went with me. They climbed trees near the Farmer's Market. They scaled fences, too.

Our volunteers were verbally attacked on many occasions, usually by those who believed us to be anti-Christian. It happened twice to me in front of a grocery store. Each time, a stranger came to my defense.

Once I obtained permission to set up a table in front of Costco. A customer started yelling at me. The store manager told me my permission had been revoked. I would have to leave.

"Why?" I asked. "There's a disturbance, but I'm not causing it!"

"How do I know that?" he replied. "Anyway, your presence is causing the disturbance and I must ask you to leave."

"That's undemocratic and unconstitutional," I told him.

I explained the *spectators veto*: anybody can drive out free speech by creating an intolerable disturbance. The courts have ruled this cannot be permitted.

As I politely argued and held my ground, a woman approached. She had seen the whole thing. I did nothing to provoke the man's tirade, she said. The manager let me stay.

After five months and countless bumps in the road, we turned in our signatures and anxiously waited to see if we had enough valid ones. We knew it would be close.

The opposition tried to sabotage our petition. People signed with fake names and addresses, giving us a false sense of how many signatures might be valid. That could also produce failure, because on the first count, the Registrar of Voters only spot-checked signatures, extrapolating the result from samples. A bad sample could lead to a bad result. Despite the difficulties, misleading information, and attempts to thwart our efforts, we collected enough signatures. Our recalls qualified for the November ballot.

The second phase of the recall proved to be much easier. Both sides had waged public opinion battles for two years. The sides became clearly defined. Few undecided voters remained.

Still, neither faction could take anything for granted. We campaigned hard for three months and won in November, 54 percent to 46 percent. Two conservative Christian trustees were recalled mid-term and removed from the Vista School Board. Moderates regained a majority, which they maintain to this day.

North County Forum
1997 - 2013

The two-year school Board battle and the Unitarian Universalist Fellowship introduced me to liberals and progressives who shared a passion for secular public education, separation of church and state, factual science, honest and age-appropriate sex education, and the importance of peace. I gained a much clearer sense of our community after talking to my fellow citizens and reading hundreds of letters-to-the-editor.

I have always enjoyed and learned from letters-to-the-editor, an effective way to reach lots of readers. Opinions in the *L.A. Times* and *Santa Barbara News-Press* informed me when I was deciding about the Vietnam War in the 60's. I hoped young people were reading them now. Our local paper published letters from both sides, true to its unique policy of printing virtually every letter that came in. In a war of ideas, truth should always beat untruth – in a fair fight.

The end of the School Board battle left me restless. I set out on a new mission: to use my organizing skills and experience to unite local liberals and progressives to make us more effective in promoting our ideals.

I discussed this with Kathy, of course, and had lunch with Carol Hilton and Dwight Smith, co-ministers of Palomar Unitarian Universalist Fellowship. They thought it was a good idea, worth a try.

In January, 1997, I wrote a letter to the editor of the *North County Times* :

> I am writing to announce the formation of North County Forum, which aims to organize liberals and promote liberal and progressive causes, education, and culture in North County. Readers can expect us to speak out and take action in favor of such things as science, reason, evolution, equality, separation of church and state, and living in harmony with nature, and against such things as immigrant bashing, gay bashing, racism, sexism, and the wanton destruction of

198

resources, habitat, and species. I also wish to announce our first annual letters to the editor contest. We will give awards in various categories for letters published in the *North County Times*.

Interested citizens contacted me and North County Forum was born!

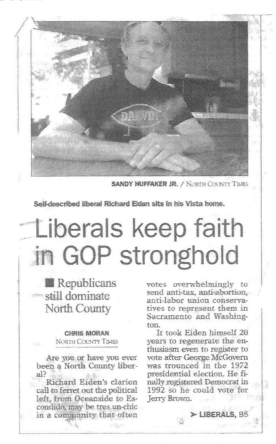

SANDY HUFFAKER JR. / NORTH COUNTY TIMES

Self-described liberal Richard Eiden sits in his Vista home.

Liberals keep faith in GOP stronghold

■ Republicans still dominate North County

CHRIS MORAN
NORTH COUNTY TIMES

Are you or have you ever been a North County liberal?

Richard Eiden's clarion call to ferret out the political left, from Oceanside to Escondido, may be tres un-chic in a community that often votes overwhelmingly to send anti-tax, anti-abortion, anti-labor union conservatives to represent them in Sacramento and Washington.

It took Eiden himself 20 years to regenerate the enthusiasm even to register to vote after George McGovern was trounced in the 1972 presidential election. He finally registered Democrat in 1992 so he could vote for Jerry Brown.

➤ LIBERALS, B5

North County Times feature article.

The next month I scheduled a poetry reading featuring San Diego's most political poet, Steve Kowit. At an organizational meeting, people expressed interest in North County Forum (NCF) and issues they felt strongly about. Both events were well-attended. Committees were formed based on areas of interest.

199

Human Rights became the most popular committee. The Letters Night idea was also popular. Kathy and her best friend helped me form the first steering committee. We quickly added promising talents to help broaden and give direction to the group. That year we held a flurry of committee meetings. People got to know each other, and we organized educational events.

The Human Rights committee surveyed local liberals on issues most important to them. The Letters committee met regularly to discuss each month's best and worst letters in the *North County Times*, and to plan the awards contest promised in my January letter.

I wanted to encourage writers whose letters-to-the-editor I had admired to come to a contest awards event. High on my list were Jeanette and Rocky Velgos, who were active in PFLAG (Parents and Friends of Lesbians and Gays). They had written letters promoting love and inclusion, with kind answers to homophobic letter writers.

Conservative Catholics, Rocky and Jeanette raised seven children in Oklahoma. Two of their children were gay. The conflict between their religious beliefs and their love for their sons produced a crisis from which they would emerge enlightened, happy, and passionate about equality for all people, regardless of sexual orientation. To maximize the chances of Rocky and Jeanette attending the awards event, I let them know that one of their letters would receive an award.

About 40 people showed up for our first Letters Night. On one hand, it was boring and unimaginative. Members of the Letters Committee sat around a table, taking turns reading the award-winning letters displayed by an overhead projector on a portable screen. On the other hand, the letters chosen had power and/or humor, making the evening a success in spite of the amateurish presentation.

The North County Times printed more than 6,000 letters each year. Some were moving, informative, well written, passionately argued – even majestic. Some were sarcastic, funny, idiotic, petty, outrageous. The newspaper had a unique policy of printing virtually every letter it received as long as it was within a 200-word limit and contained no libel, slander or obscenity. Ridiculous letters were permitted, and common. I enjoyed reading the letters section each morning and often learned something. That led me to feel there would be more than enough material for an entertaining and thought-provoking evening.

After the program, Rocky Velgos introduced himself and said, "This is a great idea but it could be done better. Do you mind if I help?"

With some theatrical experience, Rocky had ideas about how to improve our program. He started attending regular committee meetings. In short order, we named him Artistic Director – at his suggestion. This proved to be a game-changer.

One of Rocky's ideas called for voice actors to present the letters theatrically. This would replace committee members who read from a page. Rocky wanted a variety of voices to move quickly from one letter to another. They would have rehearsed their lines, and would read matching the emotion of the letter writer.

He also introduced The Overture: a 20-minute rapid-fire barrage of the best sound bites from a year's worth of letters. The Overture became wildly popular.

Now able to use vivid sentences from many letters that did not receive awards, we could average 125 sound bites, on diverse subjects, in what sounded like a call and response.

One of my favorites came from an arch-conservative:

> I would like to thank the liberal writers for the invitation to join them in a meeting of people who submitted letters to the *North County Times*. I decided to decline because I would feel like the lone hydrant at the American Kennel Club show.

Over the next 16 years, Letters Night outgrew two venues and ended up with 200 people in large community buildings and theaters. Buffet dinners, complete with beer and wine on sale, became part of the regular festivities. Our awards included Best Letter, Worst Letter, Best Satire, Writer of the Year, and, finally, Best Letter from Another

Planet. Occasionally, we presented the Most Vilified award to the liberal writer whose letters received the most negative and abusive responses. We read the best from the writers we liked and the best from their critics.

We also handed out best and worst awards for letters on the major topics: war, peace, education, women's rights, gay rights, racism, immigration, taxes. We notified the winners beforehand, hoping they would attend our Letters Night. We made several good friends this way. (We didn't invite winners of those worst awards, figuring they wouldn't enjoy themselves.)

Our annual awards were submitted in a letter-to-the-editor. Reporters sometimes attended the event, took photos, wrote stories. Several photos of our gathering appeared on the society page one year. We even gave the *North County Times* an award: Best Letters Section in the Known Universe. We named the newspaper's Letters Section a "cacophony of democracy."

The thoughtful editor of the *North County Times*, Kent Davy, attended Letters Night the year the newspaper received its award. He made a short acceptance speech.

We held our 16th and final Letters Night in 2013. The *North County Times* had just been purchased, to be merged with the *Union Tribune*. Kent Davy came to speak to us one last time. We shared the sadness of losing a fine local paper, especially one with the best letters section in the known universe.

North County Forum put on many educational and cultural events over the years. I wrote, published, and mailed out an occasional eight-page newsletter for four years – 21 issues in all – until e-mail became widespread.

We also held Alternative Independence Day on July 4th for three years. No bombs bursting in air, no rockets' red glare, no celebration of the military, no sappy enforced patriotism.

Peace groups, along with a variety of other movements and organizations, set up information and sales booths outside the Palomar Unitarian Universalist Fellowship. Inside: a full roster of speakers, panel discussions, cultural presentations. Amnesty International local #471 sold food and beverages on the patio as a fundraiser.

It was great fun for a few years, bringing good people together, and presenting good information about worthy causes.

9/11 and the New Wars

Like most people, I was stunned and disoriented after the events of September 11, 2001. For the first few days, I watched TV, read newspapers and searched online for help in sorting out my feelings and my understanding. I was reading *The Guns of August* at that time, Pulitzer Prize-winning historian Barbara Tuchman's history of the outbreak of World War I. The book helped me understand 9/11 in the context of constant political struggle, including outrageous lies, arrogance, pettiness, and callousness by world leaders. 9/11 exploded on our country like the worst thing in the world, but it was not. Unspeakable horrors have taken place around the globe and throughout history. It was, as Bill Moyers said, "a teachable moment." [1]

Within a few days I got my bearings back, mainly from online articles by people like Howard Zinn, Michael Moore, Arianna Huffington, Robert Sheer, Rabbi Michael Lerner, and Deepak Chopra. An open letter to the *New York Times* summed up my own feelings. It came from the parents of Greg Rodriguez, who was killed in the World Trade Center:

> Our son died a victim of an inhuman ideology.
> Our actions should not serve the same purpose.
> Let us grieve. Let us reflect and pray. Let us think
> about a rational response that brings real peace
> and justice to our world. But let us not as a nation
> add to the inhumanity of our times.

In a separate letter to President George W. Bush, Phyllis and Orlando Rodriguez depicted the same worry I held:

> Your response to this attack does not make us feel
> better about our son's death. It makes us feel worse. It
> makes us feel that our government is using our son's
> memory as a justification to cause suffering for other
> sons and parents in other lands. . .This is not the time
> for empty gestures to make us feel better. It is not the
> time to act like bullies.

> We urge you to think about how our government
> can develop peaceful, rational solutions to terrorism,
> solutions that do not sink us to the inhuman level of
> terrorists.

I quickly published an eight-page special issue of the North County Forum newsletter, *Voices of Reason,* excerpting various sources to urge rational reactions and restraint.

My local Congressman, Darrell Issa, held a town hall meeting two weeks after the 9/11 attacks. Friends and I attended, passing out *Voices of Reason* in the parking lot. When I tried to hand one to Issa, he became visibly angry, waved me off, then stormed inside. In his speech, he later appeared to regret his dismissal of me and the views I represented. We were attacked, Issa noted, because we are a great country. As proof, he referred to our freedom of speech, then mentioned me and the North County Forum, pointing out that our newsletter sat on the literature table in the back of the room.

I spoke out and demonstrated against our country's bombing and invasion of Afghanistan in early October, 2001. History demonstrated that Afghanistan could not be conquered or controlled from outside. Alexander the Great tried, then the mighty Roman legions, and recently the Soviet Union. All failed. Soviet states shared a border with Afghanistan. With a large and sophisticated military, the USSR withdrew all of its forces after a 10-year occupation and war. It seemed unrealistic, then, that the U.S. could do better from halfway around the planet.

And I believed our government and citizens were thinking with their emotions, not their heads. Our country had been attacked. Revenge was a natural reaction. President Bush was taking advantage of the heat of the moment to launch a war and an occupation. That, to me, was immoral, illogical, and self-defeating.

Osama Bin Laden and most of the 9/11 hijackers were Saudis, not Afghans. Still, support for an attack on Afghanistan seemed virtually unanimous. My friends thought I was "out there" by opposing this war. I felt proud that I was. I still do.

The bombing began on October 7, 2001, and the terrible war continues.

B y May, 2002, I began to suspect that Bush & Co. intended to attack Iraq. When I started spreading that concern, people thought I had finally gone off the deep end. Didn't the White House have more than enough on their hands with the unsuccessful occupation of Afghanistan? Launching a new invasion in another country would be insane, wouldn't it?

"Exactly!" I responded. "It's totally crazy! That's why we have to stop it!"

In late August, it became clear even to the doubters that the White House was preparing to attack Iraq. President Bush made a campaign appearance in Orange County with the Republican candidate for Governor. Six of us drove north to join several in the OC peace movement. We protested in front of the Monarch Beach Resort in Dana Point. It was hard to image this threat of war turning into the terrible reality we would be watching on national TV in the years to come.

The White House claimed Saddam Hussein possessed weapons of mass destruction. He had used these WMD, notably gas, against his own people. He posed a threat to the region. President Clinton had said the same things, but Bush & Co. claimed new, specific and urgent threats. The evidence was convincing, compelling.

Except, it wasn't.

For one thing, U.N. weapons inspectors had access to potential weapons sites in Iraq since George H.W. Bush's 1991 Gulf War. No WMD facilities were discovered. How could the White House claim WMDs were there now?

A handful of journalists reported that the White House was making excuses for its decision to overthrow Saddam Hussein. Reports from big media outlets ignored that angle. Was our government and the media lying in order to get us involved in another war? It seemed clear enough to many of us that truth had, indeed, become the first casualty.

The Bush administration assured us that it would be a short war, that our troops would be "greeted like liberators," and that Iraq's oil would pay for it – but these assertions, like Saddam Hussein's weapons of mass destruction, were nothing but lies.

In the years to come, official votes in Congress to support the Iraq war effort, especially the vote to empower President Bush to make the decision to go to war, would hang over the heads of a number of presidential candidates, including John McCain, John Kerry, Hillary Clinton.

The cost to date includes 4535 U.S. military personnel killed in action, 1554 contractors killed, 31,952 wounded, with 151,000 Iraqi casualties. When Afghanistan casualties are added, the totals rise: 6840 U.S. forces killed, 3481 contractors killed, 52,272 wounded, with 186,000 civilian deaths. So far, more than $6 trillion from the U.S. Treasury has gone to pay for the war. By 2015, 970,000 disability claims had been registered with the Veterans Administration. [2]

To support the false narrative of how easily and quickly the Iraq War would be won, a victory celebration was staged on May 1, 2003. After landing in a Navy S-3B Viking aircraft on an aircraft carrier off the coast of San Diego, a flight-suit clad President Bush emerged to proclaim the end of combat operations. A banner strung behind him declared *Mission Accomplished*. The incident stands as cartoonish proof of how stupid and/or dishonest the George W. Bush White House was.

During the run-up to war, our growing group of activists picketed and rallied, wrote letters to the editor, held educational events, film screenings, and poetry readings, hoping to inform and unite enough opposition to stop the war. I emailed instructions for making inexpensive signs to my North County Forum list, along with a digest of anti-war events and organizations.

The author at a street protest against the Iraq War.
North County Times: March 21, 2003

One Sunday, in church, I announced my intention to stand at a busy intersection during rush hour for the next few mornings with a sign. I invited others to join me there after church. That morning, 14 people came with me. The same number showed up the next morning, nine the next day.

We organized small weekday demonstrations on busy intersections and larger weekend demonstrations near the entrance to a local mall. Veterans for Peace began holding Arlington West events, erecting white crosses in neat rows, each with the name of a service member who had been killed in Afghanistan. Later they would add names from the Iraq invasion. Not long after that, it proved impossible to erect enough crosses for each soldier killed in both disastrous wars.

I would arrive early to help set up the crosses at the beach and in public parks. At night, we lit a candle at each cross.

A Vietnam Veteran stood with a sign in front of a local congressman's office every Tuesday at noon. Others soon joined him. During the final two months before the war, 40 people showed up each week.

Hometown Arlington West Memorial

photograph by the author

Three days before the war, I spoke at a rally at the Oceanside Pier Amphitheater. The night before the war started, we held a small candlelight vigil on a corner in downtown Vista. I read *War*, a famous anti-war poem, written during World War I by Carl Sandburg. I had the same sense of foreboding that Obie Wan Kenobi felt when the Death Star destroyed the home planet of Princess Leia in *Star Wars*:

> "I sense a great disturbance in the force, as if millions of voices cried out in terror, and were suddenly silenced."

The initial attack, called *Shock and Awe* by the White House, began the next day. Air strikes continued for days. The subsequent invasion and occupation brought more death and destruction, and unleashed anarchy and rivalries that would spread throughout the Middle East.

209

In previous wars, the official causes were based on enemy attacks, even if some of those attacks were fabricated. Iraq had not attacked the U.S. *Shock and Awe* didn't come as a response to a call for help from an ally. Instead, it was a premeditated, preemptive first strike against a wholly contrived threat.

At the end of World War II, with General Patton's Third Army battle-tested and still in the field, calls for a swift invasion of communist Russia circulated among those who, like Vice President Cheney more than a half-century later, saw an easy and fast victory over an ally believed to be a potential foe. Wiser heads prevailed then.

During the Cold War, with Moscow placing missiles in Cuba and the threat of nuclear war in the air, the same might-makes-right faction urged a First Strike to neutralize the USSR and its ICBM arsenal. Once again, wiser heads carried the day.

The Bush Doctrine – launching preemptive strikes – ignored that history.

---

[1] *Silence: the Greatest Sedition*, Moyers' keynote address for the Environmental Grantmakers Association in Brainerd, MN, Oct. 16, 2001

[2] Watson Institute of International and Public Affairs, Brown University, 2018.

Scapegoating Immigrants Again

My involvement with immigration issues began in 1974 when I worked with CASA (*Centro de Acción Social Autónomo* – Center for Autonomous Social Action). Politicians blame and crack down on immigrants every time they need a political whipping boy. Whenever no hot war or international enemy *de jure* can be found, politicians will use crime, drugs and immigration to agitate their base.

In 2005, conservative politicians revved up the propaganda machine again, claiming that immigrants were the cause of our problems – not NAFTA or globalization or automation or big banks or wars in the Middle East, not the general decay of an economic system running out of land to steal and natural resources to exploit. Anti-immigrant forces ramped up tried-and-untrue lies about immigrants and crime, immigrants and drugs, and how immigrants take our jobs.

The Republican-led House of Representatives soon passed a restrictive and punitive immigration bill. It was so controversial, even President Bush and leading Senate Republicans opposed it.

The Sensenbrenner Bill was seen as an attack on immigrants. It mobilized the Latino community. A nationwide demonstration was planned for May 1, 2006.

Called *El Gran Paro* – The Great Strike – the protest called for a boycott. Immigrants and their allies would refuse to show up to work, students would walk out of school. All would join the rallies in their towns and cities. Some called it *A Day Without Immigrants*, hoping to show how important immigrants are to our everyday lives. In Los Angeles, 500,000 demonstrators marched. In Chicago, 100,000 turned out. Protestors hit the streets across the country.

I heard that Vista High School students planned to walk out of their classrooms and march through town. I decided to join them for support. I would also act as an informal legal observer. I waited at a strip mall across from the high school. When they triumphantly emerged from school,

211

anxious to speak out for their friends, families, and for justice, I walked with them.

Rally cries and chants filled the air: "We didn't steal your jobs! We were here first!" "We didn't cross the border, the border crossed us!"

We marched around town without incident, then rallied in a small park. I took photos of colorful signs, flags, clothing, families with small children holding tiny flags, and the earnest faces of the next generation of Americans. A feeling of unity and strength pervaded that park.

The huge outpouring in so many cities and towns scared the Republicans. The Sensenbrenner Bill never passed the Senate.

The wave of Latino emotion and energy now threatened to translate into votes for Democrats. Another factor worried the Republican base: the business community. Anti-immigrant hysteria might work at election time, but the business community needed and valued those who worked hard for low wages.

Those beautiful families in the park also posed a threat to racists. Bigots had already mobilized as Minutemen, and pressured two local cities to pass anti-immigrant laws. Over the objection of the sizeable Latino community, Escondido passed a law requiring landlords to evict undocumented tenants.

Families supporting families

photograph by the author

212

Landlords opposed the new law. They didn't want the burden of checking immigration documents or risk legal liability for failure to follow the law. Some, of course, were sympathetic to the undocumented workers. The ACLU sued. Escondido, advised by its own lawyers to settle, had to pay the ACLU $90,000 in attorney fees just for filing a lawsuit. As a lifelong ACLU supporter, I loved that!

My City of Vista tried to pass an ordinance outlawing day laborers, a special target of local Minutemen. The City Council withdrew this proposal after learning that other cities had tried it, and that the proposal was found to be unconstitutional. Instead, Vista passed an ordinance prohibiting anyone from hiring day laborers within the city without a permit. To its credit, the city established an easy way to get that permit. I got one of the first.

The Vista compliance officer tried to make sure everyone hiring a day laborer had a permit, but spent some of his time as a referee between us and the Minutemen. We were there to deter and prevent the Minutemen from abusing the day laborers or overstepping their bounds in any way, and to show solidarity with the workers. The Minutemen came to oppose the presence of day laborers in the city and to make their lives more difficult. They harassed day laborers and anyone who slowed down to talk with them.

A group of observers organized to go to Vons and Home Depot parking lots on behalf of the day laborers. We felt the need to monitor the Minutemen's activities, to stand with the immigrants and to demonstrate against the hatred and scapegoating. Our presence limited their freedom to intimidate the day laborers – or worse. We held signs and counter-demonstrated so the workers and the community would see that not all Vistans were racists, while the Minutemen picketed a local Bank of America branch for doing business with immigrants without checking immigration papers.

The Minutemen staged their most ridiculous protest at a Catholic church in Fallbrook. They opposed day laborers congregating in front of the church, even though they had permission to do so. The Minutemen harassed the group. The church responded by setting up a drive-thru area on campus, complete with seating, shade, and a drinking fountain. The Minutemen couldn't get near the day laborers or interfere with their conversations with those who drove through on church property.

Foiled, the Minutemen staged larger, weekend protests on the sidewalk, aiming their anger at the church and its priest. We showed up there a few times to show support for the church and for the day laborers. I carried a sign – *What part of SCAPEGOAT don't you understand?* – as a response to the racists and GOP constant claim that immigrants were to blame for taking "our" jobs (it was mainly automation and companies moving overseas), for crime, school overcrowding, etc.

The local press carried photos and articles with interviews of people on all sides. We thought things were going well, but the Priest asked us to stop coming. To his mind, the high profile confrontations had served their purpose. The church wanted things to calm down.

Local Minuteman groups became less visible and active after a September, 2007 editorial appeared in the *San Diego Union-Tribune,* calling them "hate dispensers, intolerant bullies, maladjusted misfits, and un-American." This no doubt pissed off the Minutemen, who always made a great pretense of being patriots. I had a sign made with all four disparaging labels listed after the words *San Diego Minutemen are.* I also made half-page copies of the editorial and distributed them wherever the Minutemen assembled to spread their lies and hate.

In 2009 the Minuteman movement died out. Its members became active in the Tea Party, refused to accept the legitimacy of Barack Obama, and worked to cripple his presidency. Unfortunately, Senate Majority Leader Mitch McConnell (R – Kentucky) and other leading Republicans seem to join with racists nationwide. Senator McConnell revealed his intent to make the newly-elected Obama a one-term President. The Tea Party had a powerful ally in its single-minded effort to make Barack Obama fail as our President.

214

Anti-immigrant sentiment also died down when the Bush-Republican recession of 2008-09 hit and caused massive unemployment. The undocumented population in the U.S. dropped 10 percent within two years. Anti-immigrant sentiment would simmer on a political back burner until the 2015 candidacy of Donald J. Trump.

Occupy!

In September 2011, New York City's Zuccotti Park witnessed the birth of the Occupy Wall Street movement. The protest targeted the role the financial sector played in the steadily-growing inequity between rich and poor, and the erosion of the middle class. From NYC's financial district, the Occupy movement spread across the country. Camping in parks and public places, protesters refused to leave.

Excited by this movement's emphasis on the wealth, privilege, and power held by the top one percent, I most liked how Occupy pointed the finger of shame at both the Democratic and Republican parties. Both were responsible for the growing impoverishment, inequality and injustice in our system.

Occupy took inspiration from a worldwide upsurge protesting the lack of democracy in the Middle East, *The Arab Spring*. Austerity measures, economic crises and mushrooming inequality in Spain, Ireland, and Greece added momentum. Within a month of its original rally, Occupy had arrived in my backyard, taking over a park near the San Diego Convention Center and the lawn around L.A.'s City Hall.

October 15 became the Global Day of Action in more than 950 cities in 82 countries. By the end of the month, hundreds of Occupy sites clogged parks and public places in the U.S., with hundreds more around the world. Talk of class war filled the air for the first time since my roommates and I stuck an *EAT THE RICH* sticker on our refrigerator in 1972.

People were talking honestly about the misery of living in the greatest country, who was to blame for the inequities, what to do about it all. This struck me as the most exciting mass movement I'd seen since the good old days of the late '60s and early '70s.

Weekly solidarity protests were being staged in Oceanside, Escondido, Vista, and Encinitas, but no permanent site in North County had been established. Wanting to help plant the seeds of this movement so that its ideas would take root and grow, I thought of Occupy as a wave. I wanted to help push it forward and ride it as far as it would go.

So I decided to run for Congress.

Ocuppy DC supporters at the Supreme Court, January 2012.
photograph by Katrina Eiden

A Marine at an Occupy event in San Diego.
photograph by the author

Eiden for Congress!

At first, my strategy focused on raising local awareness on the Occupy issues and on increasing activism. Several good people encouraged me to run. We were politically *simpatico*. Or so they thought.

Some helped me get started, but soon realized I was serious about blaming Democrats as well as Republicans. We all distrusted Republicans because of George W. Bush's lies, his disastrous invasions and occupations of Afghanistan and Iraq, and for the worst economic crisis since the Great Depression. Bashing Republicans came easy. I stood as the only candidate who would speak out against both parties – for enabling the wars, for being fully conscious participants in a profoundly unjust system.

As bad as Darrell Issa might have been, I didn't aim my fire at him nearly as much as my Democrat friends wanted me to. Plenty of folks readily trashed Issa. I felt the need to point out that our whole system was at fault.

Who in Congress challenged our wars in the Middle East, our 900+ military bases in other countries, our soul-stealing military budget? Who in Congress looked beyond gun control to address the culture of violence our system created?

Kathy and I discussed my potential candidacy. Finally, I decided to run as an independent. That way, I could shine a light on both parties. If I ran as a Democrat, as Bernie Sanders would a few years later, I would not be able to tell the full truth as I saw it. Members of my original campaign committee dropped out that winter, but my independent approach attracted new supporters.

Occupy meetings and demonstrations held in local communities provided opportunities for me to talk with like-minded voters. My supporters and I handed out fliers, stood with signs on the same busy corners where we previously protested against war and racism. This time I was a candidate for public office – shaking hands, meeting people, talking about issues that mattered. It was a wonderful experience. People eagerly shared ideas about what was wrong and what could be done about it.

Maybe some of those folks thought I could win, but I knew my chances were close to zero – unless the Occupy energy kept growing until the election. It didn't.

Darrell Issa had prevailed by solid margins in five previous elections. Our Congressional district was always considered safe for a Republican candidate. I tried to raise a flag for thinking outside the box, hoping to end the charade of one corporate party pretending to be two. Would voters rally around the 99 percent and against the elite financial sector? Unsure how to rally them, I felt I had to do something. Besides, this seemed interesting and fun.

The original Occupy site in Zuccotti Park was forcibly cleared out by the NYPD on November 15th. Other cities followed suit. Winter weather made it difficult to maintain permanent outdoor sites, so fewer people were present when police came to remove them. Resistance to eviction was becoming weak and futile.

The remaining Occupiers got evicted in December after the Obama Administration coordinated a conference call with 18 big city mayors who became fed up with the disruption and the cost. Despite the evictions, the Occupy spirit remained alive. Periodic demonstrations and vigils continued worldwide for months.

Also in December, the national Occupy movement announced an *Occupy Congress!* event for January 17th. The event would lobby and demonstrate in D.C. against a corrupt political and financial system. With a focus on Tuesday the 17th, the effort would last all week. Friday, January 20th would be the second anniversary of the Citizens United ruling that allowed unlimited campaign contributions from undisclosed sources. That coming week in D.C. promised an opportunity to connect with the movement I felt so much a part of. It would also give me a chance to visit Katrina, then attending Howard University.

I struggled with the fact that the voters I was trying to persuade lived in San Diego and Orange Counties, not the

District of Columbia. Would this be a waste of several valuable days of campaigning in the district?

I connected with other San Diego activists once I got to Washington, D.C. They arranged for meetings between San Diego people and local members of Congress, and for a meeting with local homeless people and advocates. There, we learned about life on the streets – what was and wasn't being done about homelessness in D.C.

The author at the Capitol

January, 2012

The Occupy movement began with encampments in parks, town squares, and other public places that served as spaces for the homeless. One of these public places in D.C., Freedom Park, was crowded with tents, beach chairs, campfires, small grills, trash cans – and curious gawkers like me. Occupy was definitely in town!

On the big Tuesday, I spent five hours on the lawn in front of Congress talking to people from all over the world. One Canadian reporter mentioned me in his article. I also met a San Diego reporter who, after some research, wrote a very long article for an online publication about our independent campaign.

Amid creative signs and banners, information kiosks, and humor, I talked with friendly, enthusiastic people and took photos until I grew hungry and exhausted.

On Friday, Katrina joined me to protest the Citizens United decision at the Supreme Court in bitter cold. To be with her as she was finishing college and heading for law school, and to share this moment with her, was the kind of heartwarming memory a Dad never forgets.

Back home, the nuclear power plant at nearby San Onofre was discovered to have hundreds of faulty steam pipes inside a newly refurbished generator, exposing one of the seldom-mentioned vulnerabilities of nuclear facilities – plumbing.

Just a year earlier, the Fukushima earthquake and tsunami revealed what could happen. Nature destroyed the plant, releasing radiation into both the atmosphere and the Pacific. The nearby town and its surrounding area were closed, perhaps forever.

At a city council meeting in San Clemente, I spoke in favor of closing the San Onofre plant. I had consistently opposed nuclear weapons and nuclear power, and considered myself fairly well informed on the subject. Orange County anti-nuke leaders and experts also spoke that evening. We were all well received, so we decided to speak to other local city councils about the dangers posed by the defective San Onofre nuclear plant.

I didn't know what to expect when I addressed my own very conservative city council in Vista. The council members sat quietly as 11 of us, including noted experts on nuclear power and generating plants, took turns presenting information. The city council held no authority over the San Onofre plant. The council members wouldn't be ready to condemn it anyway. I urged them to form a joint committee of local cities to study the issue – a simple and sensible proposal that would be hard for them to reject.

The San Onofre plant had always been a big mystery. Specifics about it remained secret. All five Vista council members thanked us for shedding light on obscure, unknown details. The Mayor even remarked that, like so many of us, she had driven past the nuclear plant on Interstate 5 all of her life and had always wondered about it: What problems might be lurking? Should we hold our breath or put aluminum foil next to our heads as we pass? Everyone had questions, few had answers.

San Onofre's corporate secrets were protected by the Public Utilities Commission and a compliant press. Local city leaders knew virtually nothing about the plant. I was happily surprised at the reception we got when we spoke at several city councils in Orange and San Diego counties.

A year later, Edison International decided to shut down the San Onofre plant and begin the decades-long process of decommissioning. The combination of Fukushima, the cost of replacement the failed cooling pipes, and the organized opposition, proved too much. For the parent company, San Onofre became a public relations nightmare. The true nightmare – a Fukushima event in a densely-populated evacuation area, complete with potential freeway gridlock – was not being addressed.

In fact, the nuclear power industry refused to admit it might have been a mistake to erect a nuclear power plant on a beach within 20 miles of cities like San Clemente and Laguna and threatening a potential 8 million people, and built astride the Newport-Inglewood earthquake fault, and directly adjacent to one of the most traveled interstate highways in the U.S. Some trifecta these geniuses came up with.

Many of us knew the dangers lurking within the local nuclear power plant would not evaporate with Edison International's decision to shutter the reactors. We were shocked by the company's future request that taxpayers fund the dismantling process.

The author at San Onofre nuclear plant.
March 11, 2012

Independents typically garnered four percent (4%) or less of the vote in Congressional races. Our anti-establishment campaign attracted supporters and donations. In February, 2012, we hired a campaign manager and rented an office as our headquarters. I believed we were saying what needed to be said. I could see that voters were listening. We kept going.

Kathy became involved after returning from her trip to Africa. She announced months ago that my running for Congress was a crazy idea. Now, she was finally on board!

In early May, the League of Women Voters sponsored a debate between the three challengers. The incumbent, Darrell Issa, didn't show up. Way ahead in the polls, he was not about to risk making an unforced debate gaffe.

According to a new state law, only the top two vote-getters in the June primary could go on the ballot for the general election in November. This meant that independent and third party candidates had to beat a Republican or Democrat to continue after June. The other independent in our race, an unknown retired Marine lifer, surprised everyone at the debate by agreeing with me about getting out of the disastrous conflicts in Iraq and Afghanistan.

223

On Primary Day in June, Issa won with 60% of the vote. His Democrat challenger received 30% of the ballots. independent candidates earned 7% (me) and 2% (the Marine).

Our campaign ended. We felt good about fighting for peace and deep cuts in Defense spending in a very military district. I argued against the corruption of both major parties and the dog-eat-dog nature of our political and economic systems. Swimming against the tide in this conservative Congressional District, we nearly doubled the expected vote count for an independent.

Four years later, a guy named Bernie Sanders made a run for President on a platform similar to the one I had fought for. As the Occupy movement did, I labeled the oligarchy *The One Percent*. Bernie called it "the billionaire class."

Coincidence? Plagiarism? You decide.

Epilogue

THE 2016 ELECTION

Dead people generally vote for
Democrats rather than Republicans.
— RUDY GIULIANI (*State of the Union*, CNN)

We have some bad hombres here and
we're going to get them out."
— DONALD J. TRUMP (third debate)

I love Hispanics!
— DONALD J. TRUMP (on Cinco de Mayo)

Lock her up! — chant at Trump rallies

When they go low, we go high.
— MICHELLE OBAMA
(Democratic National Convention)

Why?

My life came full circle from the Civil Rights struggle and the Vietnam War of the 1960's, to the new racism, lies, and wars of the 21st Century. In the previous century, we seemed to be moving away from tribalism, monarchies, tyrants, "revealed truth," and violence as a method of settling disputes. Tragically, we began to reverse course in the 1970's.

With the amiable Ronald Reagan as cover, traditionalists turned back the clock and took revenge on peaceniks and reformers. The Cold War ramped up again, bloody conflicts were fueled in Central America, free education began to be dismantled (resulting in the dumbing-down of America), fear of drugs and crime led to increased and race-based incarceration, and immigrants and undocumented workers became prime targets again.

Meanwhile the formerly bipartisan political system broke down, paving the way for Trumpism. Violence, racism, sexism, corruption, and fascism masquerading as nationalism all returned as imminent threats from our primitive past. *Oy vey*!

Instead of thoughtful, compassionate leaders working together, we now see gangsters in business suits running things. The people with good ideas seem to have no power. Those with power just offer more of the same – war, inequality, one economic crisis after another. As I write this, pundits fear a new financial collapse, fired by deficits and an exploding national debt, trade wars, treaty violations – the hallmarks of tin-pot dictators.

And then, of course, there's global warming. . .

We have such a long way to go.

Enter the new generation of activists.

Hippies of my youth held a vision of a qualitatively better world, and after thousands of years of evolution, that finally seemed possible. The hippie ideal involved living simply and peacefully, in harmony with the rest of nature, working together to provide adequate food, housing, clothing, using productive labor to nourish our bodies and souls.

Until recently, the great majority of people throughout history had little or nothing to say about their circumstances or their society. The human species had no ability to feed, clothe or house everyone on the planet. We had few tools to understand our primitive impulses of jealousy, rivalry, conflict.

Within living memory, we have gained unprecedented knowledge and power as individuals and groups. It finally appears possible to create sustainable societies based on reason, scientific discovery, compassion, and equality. The wide gap between where our species is, and where it could be, is a tragedy I've never been able to accept. Eleanor Roosevelt put it best: "When will our consciences grow so tender that we act to prevent human misery rather than avenge it?"[1]

In dark times like these, it helps to know that people always struggle to overcome obstacles and to resist oppression, that the future is unwritten, and that we've survived dark times before. We fight back against injustice, time and again. Examples fill our history. I consider it a law of nature.

New generations are resisting oppression, injustice, and Trumpism, with unprecedented actions: huge women's marches, the Me Too movement, and an outpouring of support for immigrants and refugees fleeing poverty, violence, and hopelessness.

The year 2017 saw the first-ever nationwide march of science nerds – inspiring others about the importance of science and critical thinking. My favorite sign at the San Diego edition of this march: *Got Plague? Me neither! Thank Science!* My favorite chant: "What do we want? Scientific Progress! When do we want it? After peer review!"

Humor in dark times may be the key.

In my town of Vista, 65 consecutive Tuesday demonstrations were staged in 2017-18 against Trump and the GOP in front of the office of Congressman Darrell Issa's office. Hundreds attended each week. One of the first sitting members of Congress to endorse Donald Trump during the primaries, Issa became a logical target for protesting every stupid, racist, and dangerous thing Trump said, tweeted and did. Since Trump's election, countless acts of resistance, large and small, have been staged in this country and around the world. They work: in early 2018, Darrell Issa decided not to stand for re-election.

On November, 23, 1895, naturalist John Muir addressed a meeting of the Sierra Club:

> "The battle we have fought, and are still fighting for the forests, is part of the eternal conflict between right and wrong, and we cannot expect to see the end of it. . .So we must count on watching and striving for these trees, and should always be glad to find anything so surely good and noble to strive for."

Struggle is in the nature of things. The small struggles we wage are part the slow evolution of our species. Hopefully the arc of history does bend toward justice and progress, but it does not bend itself.

Working toward a future of peace, social justice, and living in harmony with nature has fulfilled me. I've met and joined in struggle with so many interesting and wonderful people. We've felt the joy of working in common for shared values, and we've won some important little victories!

After more than 50 years of doing this work, I still feel surges of energy and joy at peace marches, rallies for justice, activist demonstrations large and small. And I still feel comradeship for those who show up, their hearts wide open, sharing and fighting for their values and aspirations.

When I'm done, I think I'll look back on a life well lived. But I'm only 74, and I'm not done.

[1]February 16, 1946, *My Day*: syndicated newspaper column

GLOSSARY OF ACRONYMS

page numbers cite first reference in text

ACLU: American Civil Liberties Union p. 35

AIM : American Indian Movement p. 84

ASB: Associated Student Body p. 59

ASU: Arizona State University p. 41

BIA: Bureau of Indian Affairs p. 85

BPP: Black Panther Party p. 38

CASA: *Centro de Acción Social Autónomo* / Center for Autonomous Social Action p. 104

CLAC: Community Legal Assistance Center p. 122

CO: Conscientious Objector p. 31

COINTELPRO: FBI Counterintelligence Program p. 38

CORE: Congress of Racial Equality p. 25

FBI: Federal Bureau of Investigation p. 38

FSM: Free Speech Movement p. 11

HOJJ: Hall of Justice Jail p. 57

HUAC: House Un-American Activities Committee p. 12

INS: Immigration and Naturalization Service p. 105

ISA: Iranian Students Association p. 115

LAPD: Los Angeles Police Department p. 35

LSCRRC: Law Students Civil Rights Research Council p. 35

Mt. SAC: Mt. San Antonio Community College p. 22

NCF: North County Forum p. 199

NLG: National Lawyers Guild p. 41

Occupy!: the Occupy movement, opposing social and economic inequality p. 216

RCP : Revolutionary Communist Party p. 131

ROTC: Reserve Officers' Training Corps p. 45

SAVAK : *Sāzemān-e Ettelā'āt va Amniyat-e Keshvar*/National Organization for Security and Intelligence of Iran p. 116

SDS: Students for a Democratic Society p. 11

UCLA: University of California at Los Angeles p. 33

UCSB : University of California at Santa Barbara p. 19

US: United Slaves p. 38

VVAW: Vietnam Veterans Against the War p. 66

WMD: Weapons of Mass Destruction p. 4

Yippee!: Youth International Party p. 67

ACKNOWLEDGMENTS

My thanks to the many people who encouraged me and helped in writing this book, including long-time poetry teacher/coach **HARRY GRISWOLD**, memoir teachers **LISA SHAPIRO** and **AMY FRIEDMAN**, as well as **JULIE PENDRAY**, **JIM BABWE**, and **CAROL KISSIN**, who each helped edit early versions, and **REV. TOM OWEN-TOWLE** who encouraged me from the beginning and provided valuable feedback along the way.

And this book and all my activist adventures since 1978 would not have been possible without the inspiration, feedback, and support – including financial – of my wife **KATHY CANNON**, one of California's finest and most dedicated criminal defense lawyers.

CREDITS

Cover and frontispiece: *Making Peace on the Beach*
—illustration by RILEY PRATO

p. 224: *Beetle on VW bus*
—line drawing by RILEY PRATO

ABOUT THE AUTHOR

DICK EIDEN grew up in Pomona, California during the 1950's, attended and graduated from UC-Santa Barbara and UCLA Law School through the 1960s, practiced law for 25 years, based in Los Angeles and Santa Barbara, and ran for Congress as an independent in 2012.

He became an anti-war and civil rights activist during the tumultuous '60's, and served as a lawyer for activists and organizations from Southern California to Wounded Knee, from Iran to Oklahoma, and back and forth across the U.S.

He founded and led North County Forum and the Sunset Poets group in North County, San Diego. His poems have appeared in numerous journals and anthologies, most notably the *San Diego Poetry Annual*. One of his poems earned Honorable Mention in the inaugural Steve Kowit Poetry Prize.

Dick lives in Vista, California with his wife Kathy Cannon, and has three grown children and one grandchild.